BOSTON
PUBLIC
LIBRARY

JUÁREZ
The Founder of Modern Mexico

ALSO BY RONALD SYME

Illustrated by William Stobbs

Alexander Mackenzie, Canadian Explorer
Amerigo Vespucci, Scientist and Sailor
Balboa, Finder of the Pacific
Benedict Arnold, Traitor of the Revolution
Bolívar, the Liberator
Captain Cook, Pacific Explorer
Captain John Paul Jones, America's Fighting Seaman
Cartier, Finder of the St. Lawrence
Champlain of the St. Lawrence
Columbus, Finder of the New World
Cortes of Mexico
De Soto, Finder of the Mississippi
First Man to Cross America
Francis Drake, Sailor of the Unknown Seas
Francisco Coronado and the Seven Cities of Gold
Francisco Pizarro, Finder of Peru
Frontenac of New France
Garibaldi, The Man Who Made a Nation

Henry Hudson
John Cabot and His Son Sebastian
John Smith of Virginia
La Salle of the Mississippi
Magellan, First Around the World
On Foot to the Arctic, The Story of Samuel Hearne
Quesada of Colombia
Sir Henry Morgan, Buccaneer
Toussaint, The Black Liberator
Vancouver, Explorer of the Pacific Coast
Vasco da Gama, Sailor Toward the Sunrise
Walter Raleigh
William Penn, Founder of Pennsylvania
Zapata, Mexican Rebel

Illustrated by Ralph Ray

Bay of the North, The Story of Pierre Radisson

Illustrated by Jacqueline Tomes

African Traveler, The Story of Mary Kingsley
Nigerian Pioneer, The Story of Mary Slessor

MEXICO

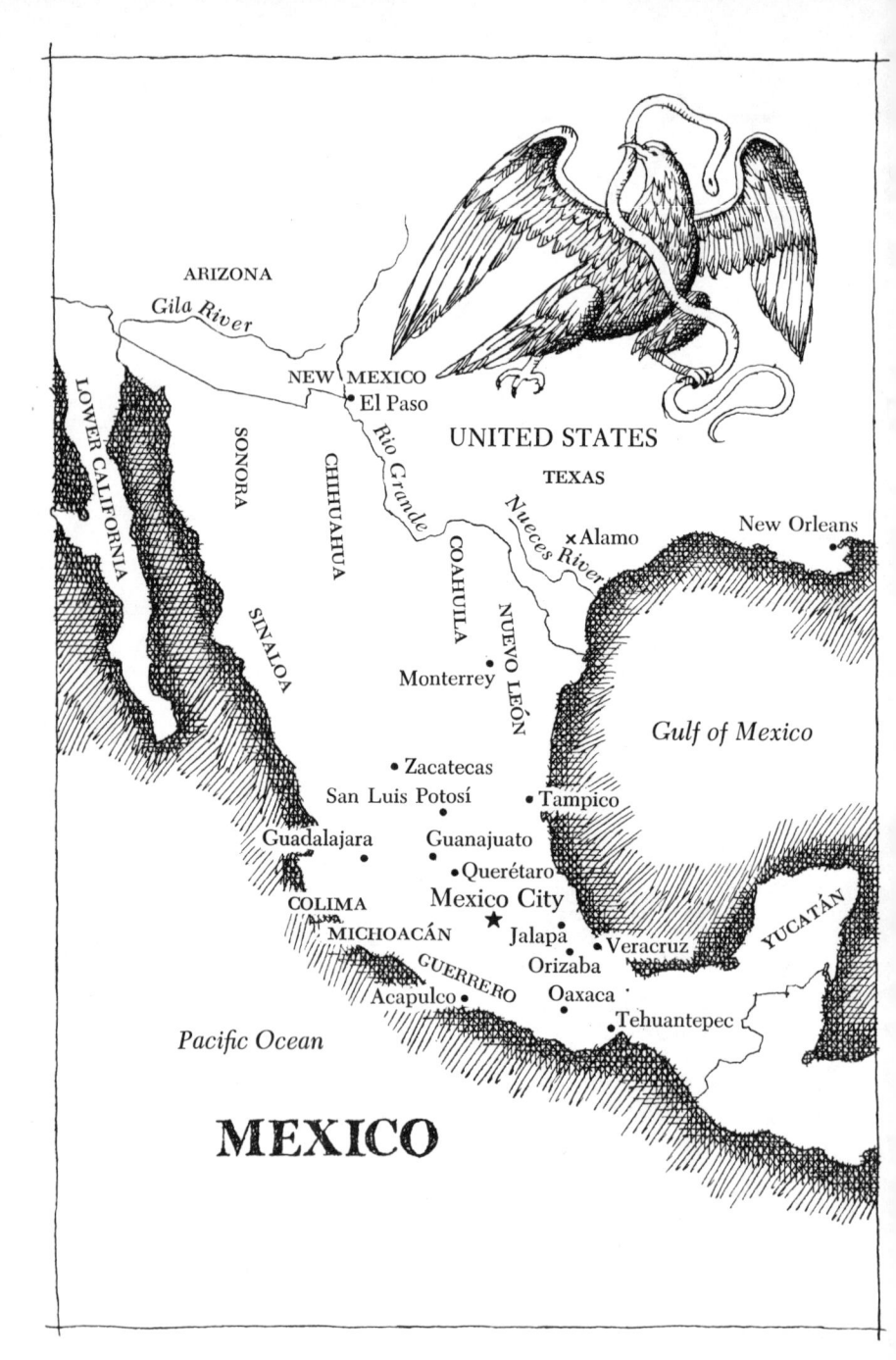

JUÁREZ
The Founder of Modern Mexico
by Ronald Syme
ILLUSTRATED BY RICHARD CUFFARI

WILLIAM MORROW AND COMPANY
NEW YORK 1972

Copyright © 1972 by William Morrow and Company, Inc.
All rights reserved. No part of this book may be reproduced or utilized in any form or by any means, electronic or mechanical, including photocopying, recording or by any information storage and retrieval system, without permission in writing from the Publisher. Inquiries should be addressed to William Morrow and Company, Inc., 105 Madison Ave., New York, N.Y. 10016.
Printed in the United States of America.
1 2 3 4 5 76 75 74 73 72

Syme, Ronald
 Juárez, the founder of modern Mexico.

 SUMMARY: A biography of the Mexican Indian, a president of his country, who instituted many reforms and overthrew Maximilian.
 1. Juárez, Benito Pablo, Pres. Mexico, 1806-1872—Juvenile literature. 2. Mexico—History—Juvenile literature. [1. Juárez, Benito Pablo, Pres. Mexico, 1806-1872. 2. Mexico—History] I. Stobbs, William, illus. II. Title.
F1233.J9545   972'.07'0924 [B] [92]   72-1544
ISBN 0-688-20031-1
ISBN 0-688-30031-6 (lib. bdg.)

Contents

1 In Search of an Education 11
2 The Texans of the Alamo 24
3 The Kidnapped Exile 39
4 A Wandering President 54
5 The Professor Becomes a General 77
6 An Emperor's Dream 96
7 The French Invaders 119
8 An Endangered Throne 139
9 Royal Tragedy 151
   What Happened Afterward 186
   Bibliography 191

JUÁREZ
The Founder of Modern Mexico

1 In Search of an Education

Under the tropical sun of Mexico the high blue mountains of Oaxaca State reach to the distant horizon. Far below the sharp-edged peaks, golden crops ripen in the green and sheltered valleys. In this vast and glittering but empty landscape, tiny whitewalled villages are isolated from the outside world and life changes little from one century to the next. Even today a man might live his entire life in the heart of those great mountains without once taking the bus that would carry him thirty miles along the winding road to the little city of Oaxaca.

Two hundred years ago, when a mule cart was a rare possession, few of the Zapotec Indian inhabitants of those forgotten mountain villages ever chose to make the journey. In their minds, Oaxaca City was a strange and wonderful place, on the fringe of a different civilization of which they knew almost nothing. It lay somewhere at the end of that dusty white road that rose and fell across the unending ranges. In tiny San Pablo Guelatao none of its score of families had ventured along those thirty miles of crumbling and arid highway to Oaxaca. They were content to spend their lives as their forefathers had done, tending their small herds of sheep and cultivating their maize and beans.

Marcelino Juárez and Grigida Garcia, his wife, were two Indians who lived in Guelatao. They were Catholics, but in spite of their Spanish names they spoke scarcely a word of that language. Their own ancient tongue was all they had ever learned. It was the only one spoken by their Indian neighbors across the ranges. The two-roomed cottage in which they lived had a floor of beaten

In Search of an Education

earth and was sparsely furnished. A *nanche* tree in the little yard outside provided a roosting place for the hens and bore cherrylike fruit in great crimson bunches.

Benito Pablo Juárez was the third child in this simple household. He was born on March 21, 1806, when his two sisters, Maria and Rosa, were already old enough to spin cotton yarn and carefully weave *rebozos*, the traditional blue or yellow shawls of the Zapotec women.

By the age of three, Benito was an orphan. His parents had died within a few months of each other. He was taken into the house of his grandparents, a few miles away, where he lived until he was about eleven years old. Then Pedro Juárez and Justa Lopez also died. Juárez went to a tiny hamlet five miles down the road to live with an uncle. His two sisters had already married and moved away to live in other parts of the state.

In later life, Juárez was to remember Uncle Matias for the advice and help he was able to give. Matias was only a small peasant farmer, but he was also a far-seeing man.

"Times are going to change in Mexico," he said to Juárez. "The day will come, before you're much older, when a knowledge of Spanish will be necessary to any of our people who want to get on in the world. When I was your age, I worked in the household of a merchant in Oaxaca, and I learned a smattering of the language. I'll teach you what I know. But if you want to get a better education, you'll have to go to the Catholic fathers."

The idea of becoming a priest did not appeal to Benito Juárez, but he was eager to learn as much as he could. Uncle Matias tried to help him, but his own learning was very limited, and the time seemed to pass too quickly. Forty years later Juárez wrote:

> I decided before very long that only by going to the City could I learn anything more. I often asked my uncle to take me there but he always replied, "We'll go there someday," but he never made a move to begin the journey.

A simple misfortune settled the matter very quickly. One day, when he was guarding sheep on a nearby hillside, he met a party of men traveling along the road with some mules they had bought. Juárez discovered that they came from

Oaxaca City and were on their way back there now. He asked them to tell him something about the place and, while listening attentively, he forgot about the sheep.

After the muleteers had gone off down the road, Juárez counted his flock. One of the sheep was missing. Another shepherd on an adjacent hillside told him why.

"Those men held your attention most cunningly," he said. "You never saw one of them circle round behind your back and grab the animal. He was off with it before I could get down here to warn you. You'll never be able to overtake them now."

Juárez was unable to decide in later years whether it was his fear of Uncle Matias's temper or his own ambition that made him decide to run away.

At any rate he never went back to the farm. As a slender, dark-skinned, ragged boy only twelve years old, he began to walk along the road that led to the distant city. He reached the outskirts of Oaxaca before nightfall.

It was fortunate for him that his sister Rosa had decided to leave her husband a year or two earlier. She had come to Oaxaca and was employed as a cook in the house of a wealthy, part-Italian family. She was surprised to see her young brother arrive, but she did what she could for him. During the next few nights Juárez slept in a shed in the kitchen yard, protected from the cold with a few old potato sacks. He ate with the servants in the kitchen, puzzling over their speech, a strange mixture of Indian dialect and Spanish.

During the day Juárez wasted no time. He had arrived in Oaxaca, and now it was up to him to make his way in a new and strange world. The city itself was a disappointment. It had a convent and a cathedral, several churches, and a few straggling streets lined on both sides with ramshackle shops. Most of the churches, the Army barracks, and even the cathedral were grimy, and their solid stone walls had been cracked by numerous earthquakes. The central plaza was overgrown with weeds and littered with rubbish. The unpaved streets were muddy and strewn with garbage. Mosquitoes bred in stagnant pools among neglected ruins. Perhaps Oaxaca was the fringe of the civilized world, as the Zapotec Indians of the

In Search of an Education

mountains declared, but it was certainly a very grubby one.

Juárez found a job for himself in the home of Don Antonio Salanueva, a bookbinder and bookseller by trade, who was also a staunch member of the Catholic Church. This elderly man kindly went to much trouble to persuade the priest who ran the Royal School to accept Juárez as a pupil.

Within a few weeks Juárez decided that this grim-walled, damp and dreary establishment was going to be of no use to him.

> Poor boys such as I were packed into a separate room of a man who called himself the Assistant. He was useless as a teacher and as severe and quick-tempered as the headmaster. It didn't take me long to make up my mind to leave this miserable school and to try to teach myself from then on.

Juárez was encountering for the first time some of the disadvantages of being an Indian in a country where everything was made easy for the children of wealthy Spanish families who had settled in Mexico. After them came the Creoles, or families of Spanish blood who had been born in

Mexico. No one was interested in the Indian children. They were left alone to get on as best they could.

While Juárez was making forlorn efforts to educate himself in an attic high under the Salanueva roof, where he shivered at night and sweated by day, he began to notice the solemn young men who attended the Seminary every day in order to receive their training. Although he still disliked the idea of becoming a priest, he envied these students the education they were receiving. They had pens and paper, and sometimes they even carried leatherbound books. They would have scorned his scraps of paper, his battered notebook, and the crude stump of pencil he used. Perhaps Uncle Matias had been right, Juárez reflected, and he would have to attend a church school to receive a proper education. He decided to discuss his problems with Don Salanueva.

The old bookseller was pleased. "Then you must become a member of our Church," he said. He began to arrange everything, omitting only to inquire as to Juárez's own feelings at the prospect of training for the priesthood. Toward the end

In Search of an Education

of 1821, when Juárez was fifteen years old, he was allowed to attend the Seminary.

This unlovely stone building overlooked the main plaza. When the students met any of the black-robed teachers, they were expected to bow respectfully and stand aside. With its bare classrooms and barred windows, the place could have been a prison.

The education Juárez received was inadequate in many ways. He did learn to speak, read, and write Spanish, which fulfilled one of his principal ambitions, but arithmetic was almost unknown, and history was regarded as a dangerous subject to teach impressionable young men. Geography was almost entirely neglected. It was confined to a chart that showed the Atlantic Ocean, the Spanish colonial empire in the Caribbean Sea, and Mexico, which was part of that empire. The United States was merely an unmarked coastline. The rest of the world was simply omitted. In their allusions to the United States the teachers said little except that it was an English-speaking country inhabited mainly by people who were, very regrettably, members of the Protestant faith.

In his time at the Seminary, Juárez acquired a smattering of philosophy and formed the habit of making long speeches to himself in his newly acquired Spanish. He got a cheap Spanish arithmetic textbook from Don Salanueva and taught himself how to add, subtract, multiply, and divide.

The longer Juárez attended that dreary Seminary, the more he disliked the prospect of becoming a missionary to the Indians, destined to spend the rest of his life in an isolated mountain village. Oaxaca was large enough, at least, to have given him a taste for the outside world.

It was just unfortunate that the Church insisted that every student who attended the Seminary become a priest. The best Juárez could do was to spin out his education for as long as possible. He hoped that some miracle would give him the opportunity to find more pleasing employment elsewhere.

Using one excuse after another, and studying hard in the meantime, Juárez managed to stay on at the Seminary until he was twenty-one. In 1827, he passed a strict examination in philosophy

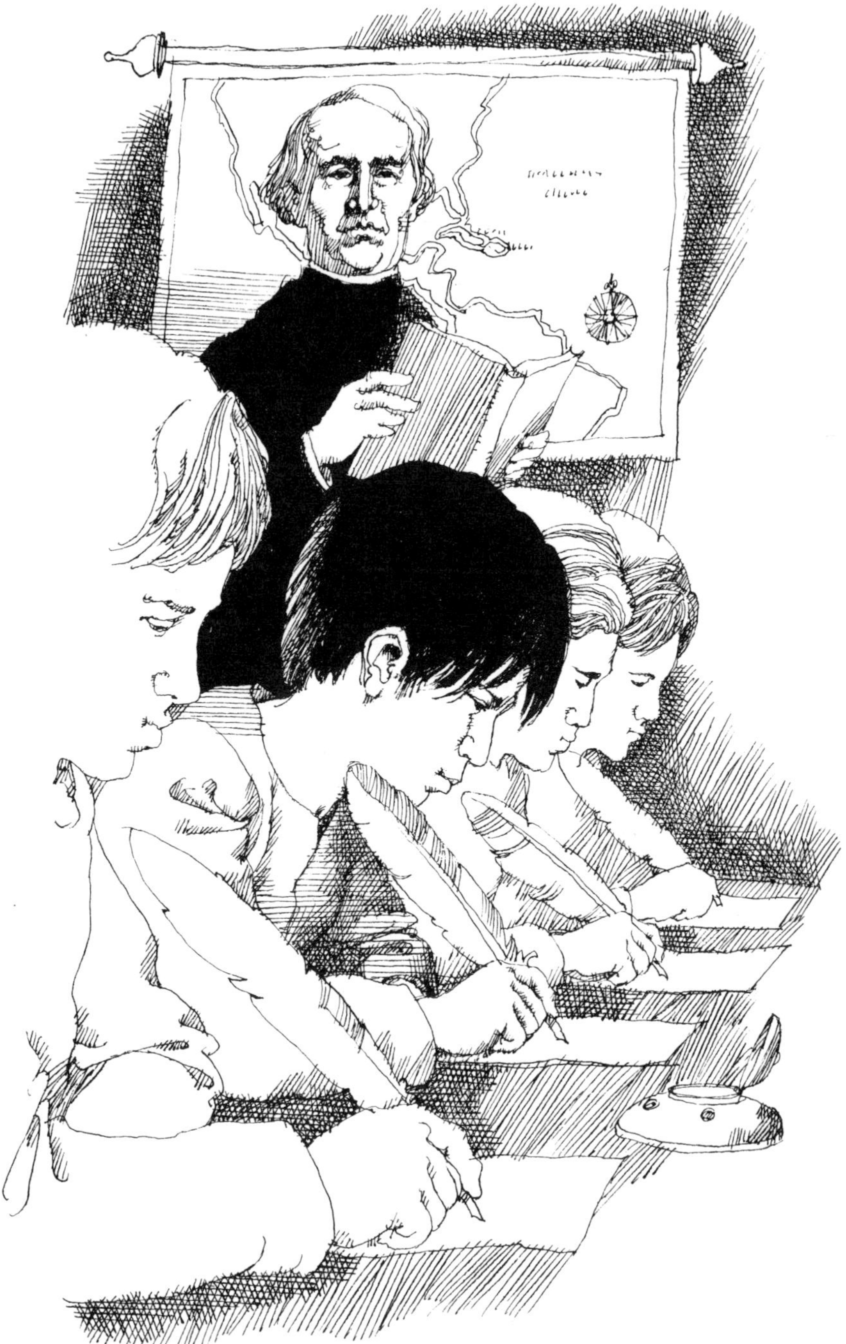

In Search of an Education

with the rating of Excellent. Now he was forced to reach a decision.

Outside Mexico City there were almost no opportunities for a young man such as myself, an Indian of obscure family, to enter any profession or business. The Spanish occupied every worthwhile post. I was faced with the fact that I must either join the Church, for which I felt myself to be unsuited, or return to my native village of Guelatao.

But Juárez was saved at the last moment. Almost entirely unknown to him, or to any of the other students at the Seminary, dramatic events were taking place in history. Mexico was already on the brink of the greatest period of change the country had known since the Spanish Conquest.

SANTA ANNA

2 The Texans of the Alamo

Kindled by the American Revolution, the flames of rebellion had spread across the world and now were reaching Mexico. While Juárez was still a child, the missionaries Father Hildalgo and Father Morelos had led unsuccessful attempts to win Mexico's freedom from Spain on behalf of the Creoles and Indians. Then, on September 21, 1821, the Mexican Spaniards themselves declared independence in order to avoid democratic political reforms that were being forced on the Bourbon King Ferdinand in Spain.

• The throne of Mexico was offered to King Ferdinand or to any of his relatives who might have discovered that democratic control of their actions was tedious. In Mexico, of course, there would be no such control. A king and the powerful individuals who supported him would be able to govern as they pleased. Any opposition to this state of affairs would be swiftly exterminated.

The royal Bourbon family of Spain hastily refused the Mexican offer. The troubles they had endured in the past few years had developed their instinct for scenting danger before it was too late.

The throne was then offered to a young Creole Army officer named Agustin Iturbide, who had played a leading part in the defeat of Father Morelos. Lacking the Bourbon instinct of self-preservation, Iturbide happily accepted the offer. Even his political opponents were so caught off guard by this sudden independence of Mexico that they promised Iturbide their loyal support. Thus upheld, Iturbide set about making the most of his royal career.

Unfortunately, Iturbide apparently was an accomplished swindler of Army contractors. Among those whom he swindled, he had the folly to include a number of the wealthy and powerful. The victims protested loudly to Congress, which protested to Iturbide himself. Angered by this interference with his royal rights, the emperor had a number of the members of Congress dumped into the local prisons. This action was too highhanded for the Army, however, which promptly revolted, with the assistance of the disillusioned supporters of Fathers Hidalgo and Morelos.

Iturbide was dethroned and banished from Mexico in 1823. He tried to return to the country a year later, whereupon he was taken prisoner and shot.

After this disappointing experiment, the men who represented Mexico's vested interests and the leaders of the Church seemed to lose their confidence. A new and more democratic Congress was hurriedly elected, and its members set about composing a fresh Constitution. As their model, the Mexicans chose the American Constitution, which appeared to be functioning very well. At the same time, this new Congress chose for the national flag of Mexico the green favored by Hidalgo, the red of Morelos, and the white flag of truce.

Inspired by their perusal of the American Constitution, the Congress of 1824 decided that the Church's monopoly on education in Mexico must end. Government schools and colleges should be opened as soon as possible. In 1827, when Juárez was reluctantly preparing to enter the Church, a new Civil College was created in Oaxaca, the Oaxaca Institute of Arts and Sciences.

At least half the students attending the Seminary deserted it at once and hurried to join the College. Among them was Juárez.

"Whether I did so out of curiosity, or because most of my companions were doing likewise," he said later, "I am not sure. But I do know that I was utterly bored with my studies of theology and its complicated principles."

The teaching staff at the Institute were all men of broadminded views. Several admitted their support of the democratic theories that Morelos had preached. Interference with the Church's monopoly angered its authorities as much as the hasty departure of many of their students. They began a vicious, slanderous campaign against the new college in sleepy, provincial Oaxaca. The lies that were told alarmed many parents so that they withdrew their sons.

A very few students stayed on, and Juárez was one of them. After struggling for years to get a decent education, he was being offered one by men who were qualified to teach. He refused to be intimidated by the jealous priests and began to study science, law, political economy, and world history. He was quickly recognized by the teachers as an outstanding student. In 1831, when he was twenty-five years old, he passed his final examinations as a lawyer with exceptionally high marks.

During the years that Juárez was a student, the plight of Mexico steadily worsened. One president succeeded another with dismal monotony. Elections remained a farce, and the violence that always accompanied the choice of a new president increased as many Spaniards either left the country or were deported. The Creoles were being left alone to fight among themselves for coveted positions within the government. Some of those early presidents saw very clearly that so long as the

Church remained all-powerful in Mexico, the country would never prosper. Such men were aware that the Church was the greatest capitalistic institution in Mexico. It completely controlled the few struggling banks. It drew vast profits yearly from its own mines. It owned enormous tracts of land and whole blocks of commercial property in the towns. Yet, in spite of all this wealth and an enormous yearly income, the Church paid no taxes to the government. Its priests were immune to Mexican law, and its secret agents were always waiting in the shadows to foment trouble for any politician who threatened to reduce its control of national life. Any president who wished to remain in office had to submit to the dictatorship of the Church, which utterly opposed all change in the country, preferring to leave the national way of life as it had been for the past three hundred years. Thus, when Juárez finally left the Institute, the unfortunate teachers had been worn down by hostile and unrelenting pressure and were becoming afraid to teach any subjects except those of which the Church approved.

Juárez, a slender and silent young man with a keen mind, knew very well what was going on.

Still, he kept his thoughts to himself, for he had his own way to make in the world. He had made up his mind that he was going to climb and, until he reached the top, did not care to risk the opposition of powerful enemies.

In 1834, Juárez was elected as a member of the legislature of Oaxaca State. The position gave him a chance to see the chaotic condition of the country at first hand.

For the past three centuries, Mexico had been exploited and stripped of its natural resources by the Spanish conquerors and their descendants. During all those years they had omitted to build up any new and worthwhile economic exports and forbidden all trade with any other country except Spain. Now the silver mines were crumbling. The machinery used for the extraction of ore was obsolete. Industry was primitive. Roads were dilapidated and few in number. Except for a few newly founded colleges such as the one in Oaxaca City, government schools of any kind did not exist. Even the rich soil of Mexico, which could have been the country's greatest asset, was cultivated by crude and wasteful methods. Forests of trees, useful for preventing erosion, had been ruined by wandering herds of goats, which nibbled away the bark and young shoots. The lack of foreign markets made the large-scale production of crops a time-wasting and unprofitable business. Corruption and inefficiency alone would have kept Mexico a poor country. Many of the government clerks could read and write only with difficulty.

When Juárez became a member of the legislature in Oaxaca, General Santa Anna had been the president of Mexico for one year.

Antonio López de Santa Anna Perez de Lebrun was the son of wealthy Spanish parents, but he had been born in Mexico. He ranked, therefore, as a Creole. Santa Anna realized that if he wanted to remain president, he would have to remain on good terms with the Church. While all over the country, junior politicians, with Juárez among them, were cautiously in favor of land reform, economic development, and justice in the courts, Santa Anna continued to preserve the status quo. This stagnancy inevitably caused fresh uprisings, although it was the last thing he wanted.

More at home in a cavalry saddle than in the president's chair, Santa Anna set off with the troops to suppress revolts in the states of Zacatecas and Coahuila. In pursuit of rebels he entered Texas, which in those days was a vast area of frontier territory lying between the United States and Mexico.

When Santa Anna arrived with his troops, the Texans feared that they were about to suffer some kind of invasion. They seized their rifles and prepared to defend themselves and their homes. The abandoned chapel of the Mission San Antonio de Valero, a lonely, crumbling building, stood in a grove of cotton trees, whose Spanish name, *álamo*, gave the chapel its name. In this improvised fort, 180 Texans under Colonel James Bowie and William Travis held off Santa Anna's 4000 troops for twelve days. When the chapel was finally captured, Santa Anna, enraged by the loss of nearly 1500 men, ordered the immediate execution of all the Texan prisoners.

In retaliation, a strong force of Americans overtook Santa Anna in San Jacinto early in 1836. They shot the Mexicans to ribbons and took the trembling Santa Anna prisoner.

The Mexican president extricated himself from this misfortune by hurriedly recognizing the in-

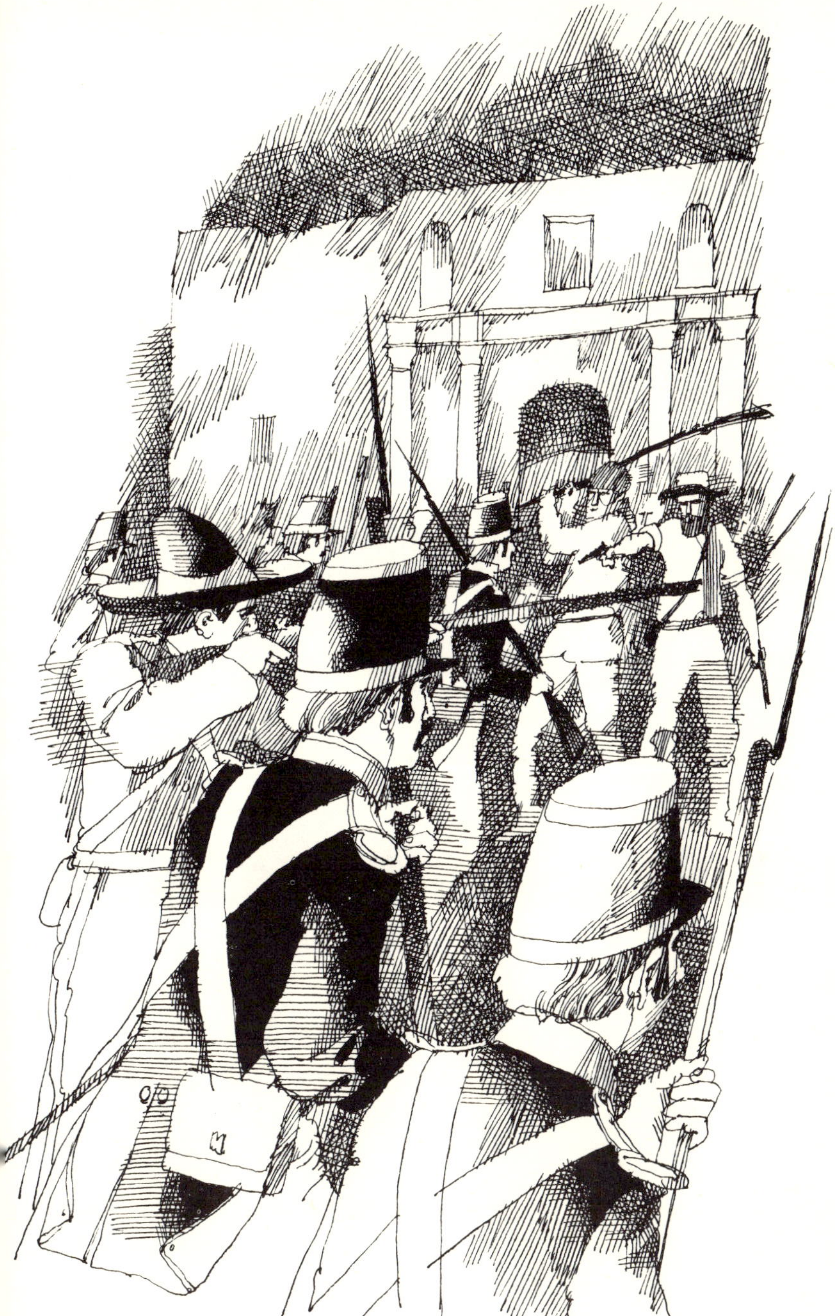

dependence of the Republic of Texas. He was released—probably much to his surprise—and allowed to hurry back to the safety of his country home in Mexico.

Santa Anna contrived to restore himself in his nation's eyes, but in 1843 his mismangement made it necessary for him to leave Mexico in a great hurry for temporary sanctuary in Havana. There he settled down to await a more favorable opportunity for his reentry into Mexican politics. As an expert gambler, he was aware that the luck of the cards was bound to change.

In remote Oaxaca, Juárez was quietly strengthening his own position. He had been admitted to the bar in 1834. In 1842, he was made a judge in the civil court. In 1843, when he was thirty-seven years old, he married Margarita Maza, the daughter of the house in which he had found shelter twenty-five years earlier as a runaway boy.

After his marriage, Juárez's leisurely climb toward fame and power became swifter. He accepted a position as secretary to the governor of Oaxaca State in 1844. Only a year later, however, he resigned when he was called upon to sign an order from the governor directing the courts that all those peasant farmers who refused to pay tax to the Church should be prosecuted. His action was approved by the more liberal-minded members of the legal profession, and a few months later he was elected as a judge to the Supreme Court, the only Indian who had ever achieved such a distinguished position. Soon afterward he was also elected to the Departmental Assembly, as the local legislature of Oaxaca was known.

Although careful how he expressed his opinions in public, to his friends in private he said:

> Our ship of state is still drifting. Soon it is going to strike the rocks. The shock of that collision is going to awaken our people as they have never been awakened before. When that happens, I think that those of us who are Liberals and believe in democratic progress, justice, and a more equal distribution of wealth may make more headway than ever before.

The Mexican Government continued to stagnate while drifting deeper into bankruptcy. Not even the foreign loans successive governments managed to raise were spent prudently. The money was merely used to pay the most urgent national debts. Meanwhile, the Mexican people were still unhappy over the loss of Texas. They refused to admit that they had lost that territory for good until it was annexed by the United States in 1845. It was the Mexican reluctance to agree that the Rio Grande now formed the boundary between their country and the United States that precipitated the long-threatened Mexican-American War. Mexico claimed, with some justice, that the border was at the Nueces River, while the Americans asserted that it was the Rio Grande.

President James K. Polk might have avoided this miserable war if he had been in less of a hurry to seize California. But Polk was a Southern slave owner, and it was assumed that any new territory acquired from Mexico would be slave territory. Besides, Polk had grown exasperated with the Mexicans in their previous dealings. In January, 1846, he ordered General Zachary Taylor's troops into the disputed area between the Nueces and the Rio Grande, with orders to defend themselves on the least provocation. The first clash between Mexicans and Americans occurred in April, and the United States Congress declared war in May.

Gomez Farias, a former vice-president of Mexico under Santa Anna, hurriedly made plans for his old chief to be brought back from Havana. Despite his weaknesses, Santa Anna had a dramatic personality that enabled him to rally the Mexican people. By July, 1846, two months after the war began, Santa Anna was in Veracruz to receive a public welcome. In December he was elected to the presidency, with Gomez Farias again installed as his vice-president.

Realizing that he desperately needed outstanding men in his Congress, Santa Anna called upon the different states to elect the best candidates they could. Men of somewhat liberal views would be preferable, added Santa Anna. Mexico must be united to face the threatening American invasion, and the way to do so was to introduce social reforms.

It was not surprising that Juárez, who was known throughout Oaxaca as a convinced Liberal, was elected to Congress by a heavy majority early in the year 1847. He now made his first journey to Mexico City, moving up the slippery ladder of Mexican politics.

3 The Kidnapped Exile

General Zachary Taylor had little enthusiasm for the war in which he found himself engaged. He admired the fierce courage of the best Mexican soldiers, at the same time disapproving of a government that could send such men into battle with worn-out muskets, obsolete equipment, and inadequate rations. Thus, his progress southward into Mexico was cautious and not as swift as it might have been. President Polk then ordered

General Winfield Scott to land a second army at Veracruz and march upon Mexico City.

The people of Veracruz held out for three weeks, which was much longer than anyone had expected. At the end of March, 1847, Scott at last began his march toward the capital. At Cerro Gordo on April 18, the Americans ran into heavy fighting, when teen-age boys from Mexico City took their places beside the last available Mexican troops. Nevertheless, a few days later the Americans entered the capital and the war was over.

A treaty between America and Mexico was signed on February 2, 1848. By its terms, Mexico ceded to the United States the territory that now comprises the states of New Mexico, Colorado, Utah, Nevada, Arizona, and California. In return the United States agreed to pay Mexico $15,000,000.

Throughout his term in Congress Juárez had remained silent. Realizing that the war must end soon, he refrained from making any speeches, either critical or patriotic, regarding it. Silence in Congress was as admired as it was unusual. Juárez earned his reward by being chosen provisional governor of Oaxaca in November, 1847. At last he had a chance to demonstrate to the whole of Mexico what could be done by an honest and democratic administration. He would make of Oaxaca State a showplace for the nation.

It was unfortunate that one of Juárez's first actions was to refuse Santa Anna sanctuary in Oaxaca. Again fleeing from a government and nation that had thrown him out, Santa Anna never forgave Juárez for what he termed "an act of insolence." He declared to his friends:

> It is amazing that an Indian who once waited on me at a dinner party in Oaxaca City many years ago, and was then clad only in a coarse linen tunic and pants, should now be in a position to treat me in such a high-handed way.

In Havana he continued to brood over the incident while awaiting the day when he could secure his revenge.

The civil administration of Mexico normally provided easygoing jobs for those who were lucky enough to obtain them. Employees did not have to pass any examinations to secure promotion. As long as a man knew the right people, he could rise quickly to a senior post. Once an employee had been taken on, he was not expected to do more than a minimum of work, while an intricate system of graft provided all state officials with additions to their salaries. Work was performed sloppily and records were in hopeless confusion, for the filing systems were inefficient and disorganized.

This state of affairs would not do for Juárez. He began to reform the civil administration of Oaxaca State within his first week in office, declaring:

> From now on all State employees will be in their offices by nine o'clock in the morning. No employee will leave at night before his desk is tidy and all papers filed in proper order. All new applicants will be required to pass an entrance test for ability and educational qualifications. Any official caught accepting a bribe or illegally altering any official document will be tried in Court and imprisoned if found guilty.

The Kidnapped Exile

Juárez then turned his attention to education. Though Oaxaca was almost bankrupt, he somehow raised the funds to build a number of schools throughout the state. He gave generous financial assistance to the Institute in Oaxaca, which he himself had attended as a student and later taught at as a professor, and opened two other colleges in backward areas where they were badly needed. He even founded a few schools for the education of women, an idea unheard of in Mexico.

Agriculture was the next project on Juárez's list of priorities. During the disturbances of past years, many small farmers had despaired of selling their crops. They had formed the habit of growing only enough to feed their own families. Yet in the deep, dark volcanic soil of those valleys, an enormous profusion of agricultural produce could be grown under almost perfect conditions.

"We cannot expect our peasants to grow crops they have no means to export," said Juárez. "Before we can bring our state into full agricultural production, communications with the outside world must be created."

He began the building of a road across a hundred miles of mountainous country to the abandoned and crumbling port of Huatluco. Almost without money and entirely lacking even the most primitive earth-moving machinery, he built the road with volunteer gangs of sturdy, patient, and indefatigable Indians.

Even the Church authorities became interested in this creation of a highway to the coast. Although normally they were suspicious of innovations and progress, they gave Juárez valuable assistance. All along the proposed route, parish priests called upon the young men of their villages to offer their services. As the road began to drive westward across the hills, a great and almost fanatical enthusiasm for it grew among the people. For the first time in the history of Mexico, the Church was actively assisting in the development and progress of the country.

The road was completed. Along it began to move the farm carts of the people, bearing loads of corn, tobacco, and cotton. Along unfinished wooden wharves and in primitive boats these exports were conveyed to ships at anchor in the bay. Meanwhile, priests and foremen ashore combined to encourage the toiling gangs of workmen

The Kidnapped Exile

to complete the renovation of the harbor as quickly as possible.

On the day that the port was completed, crowds of ragged workers and vestured priests shared the enthusiastic celebrations.

At the end of his first three years in office, Juárez was reelected by an enormous majority. Down from their remote homes in the mountains came great numbers of Zapotec Indians, bringing small gifts of fruit and fowl as offerings to their distinguished countryman. Juárez welcomed them in his governor's palace, made sure that they were fed, and let them sleep on floors and in corridors of the building. Next morning every Indian returned to the mountains, taking with him a small sum of money presented by Juárez himself.

The next two years brought even more progress to Oaxaca State. Exports grew steadily in volume, and government finances improved so rapidly that bankruptcy was left far behind. The civil administration, warned by a few severe examples Juárez made of dishonest or incompetent officials, became honest and efficient. By 1851, the prosperous condition of Oaxaca was arousing admiration and envy throughout Mexico. In that same year, Juárez built several more schools in the remote regions inhabited by the Indians. For the first time in Mexican history, these neglected and impoverished people could obtain a free education. The Church offered to supply a number of teachers, even though the subjects being taught in those new schools included geography and elementary agricultural science, which it had always ignored in its own system of education.

"I am an Indian and I do not forget my own people," Juárez had said shortly after his successful reelection. "It is my intention to give our race the opportunities that have been denied them for centuries, so that they may look forward to a better life in the years ahead."

To the north of Oaxaca, the governor of the western state of Michoacán, Don Melchior Ocampo, was greatly impressed by the progress Juárez was making. Ocampo was a wealthy Creole. Although he owned vast and valuable estates, he was progressive in his outlook. He strongly disapproved of the unlimited power of the Church. Unlike silent Juárez, who never revealed his democratic beliefs in public, Ocampo expressed his disapproval openly. His wealth and his position

The Kidnapped Exile

as a great landowner made him careless of public opinion. It was therefore not surprising when, in 1850, the Federal Government dismissed him from his post in Michoacán. Ocampo was accused of being a revolutionary and a dangerous crank who was out to harm the Church. Before his dismissal, Ocampo had begun to introduce social and economic progress in Michoacán along the lines that Juárez was demonstrating in Oaxaca.

In 1852, Juárez retired from office. He left behind him the most prosperous and best-run state in the whole of Mexico. He returned to his law practice, which by this time was prospering, and for several years he took no further part in public life. Once again, perhaps, his shrewd instincts warned him that another dangerous crisis was approaching in Mexico.

In 1853, Lucas Alamán became president as the result of another Army mutiny. Quiet and studious, Alamán came of a wealthy Creole family. After spending some years as a politician, he had retired to his country estate to write a history of Mexico.

Considering his aristocratic background and cultivated upbringing, it is not surprising that

Alamán firmly believed in a Mexico where the old order should be preserved forever. He supported the Church, disapproved of democracy, and saw no advantage in a more equable distribution of the national wealth. Any reforms intended to improve the conditions of the Mexican people, he regarded as dangerous, if not revolutionary. As far as he personally was concerned, Mexico was an excellent country in which to live. Alamán was an honest man who genuinely believed in the rightness of his principles.

When he became president, Alamán realized that he was not the right man to lead the country back into its former state, although he believed that this step should be taken. In Oaxaca and Michoacán at least, the people were practicing some dangerously democratic ideas; every man had been given the right to vote, agricultural cooperative societies were springing up, and efforts were being made by the authorities to combat the power of the priests. Such conditions must not be allowed in the Mexico that he, Alamán, intended should revert to the aristocratic rule it had known in the days of the Spanish Conquest.

There was only one man at that time with the

The Kidnapped Exile

energy, ruthlessness, and cunning to bring about these reforms. In 1853, Alamán wrote to Santa Anna, who was still living in exile, and invited him back to Mexico. In his letter Alamán explained the reforms he had in mind and which he would expect Santa Anna to enforce.

> The man really responsible for the present disturbed conditions of our country is the former governor of Michoacán, Don Melchior Ocampo. He has made it clear that he does not believe in the divine right of the Catholic Church. He is opposed to the custom that entitles priests to obtain money from their villagers. He is a severe critic of the undoubted rights of the largest landowners in his state. We believe in the necessity of maintaining the Catholic religion in splendor and in supporting the property of the Church. We are against the representative system by means of elections as they have been practiced, and against everything that goes by the name of popular elections until they rest on a different foundation.

After expressing these harsh views, which would effectively have put the clock back at least a hundred years, Alamán thought it necessary to add, "It is not true, however, that we desire the return of the Inquisition or persecutions."

Santa Anna came swiftly. One of his first steps was to draw up a list of those people whom he regarded as public enemies. Among them he recalled the slender little Indian, Juárez, the erstwhile governor of Oaxaca, the man who once had had the impudence to refuse entry to that state to someone of more distinguished birth and upbringing than himself.

Juárez was engaged in a law case in a lonely village in the high sierras outside Oaxaca State on May 27, 1853. A detachment of cavalry suddenly appeared in the narrow street. A passport was handed to him, and he was ordered to mount a horse. With the troops as escort, he was taken eastward across Mexico to the town of Jallapa in the state of Veracruz, and there he was placed in a prison cell for seventy-five days. During that time he was given no explanation for this kidnapping, nor was he allowed to communicate with his family in Oaxaca City. The military escort then reappeared, and he was taken southward in a coach to the port of Veracruz. For the next twelve days he was kept in an underground prison cell until ordered to repack the small suitcase he had with him when first arrested. At last Juá-

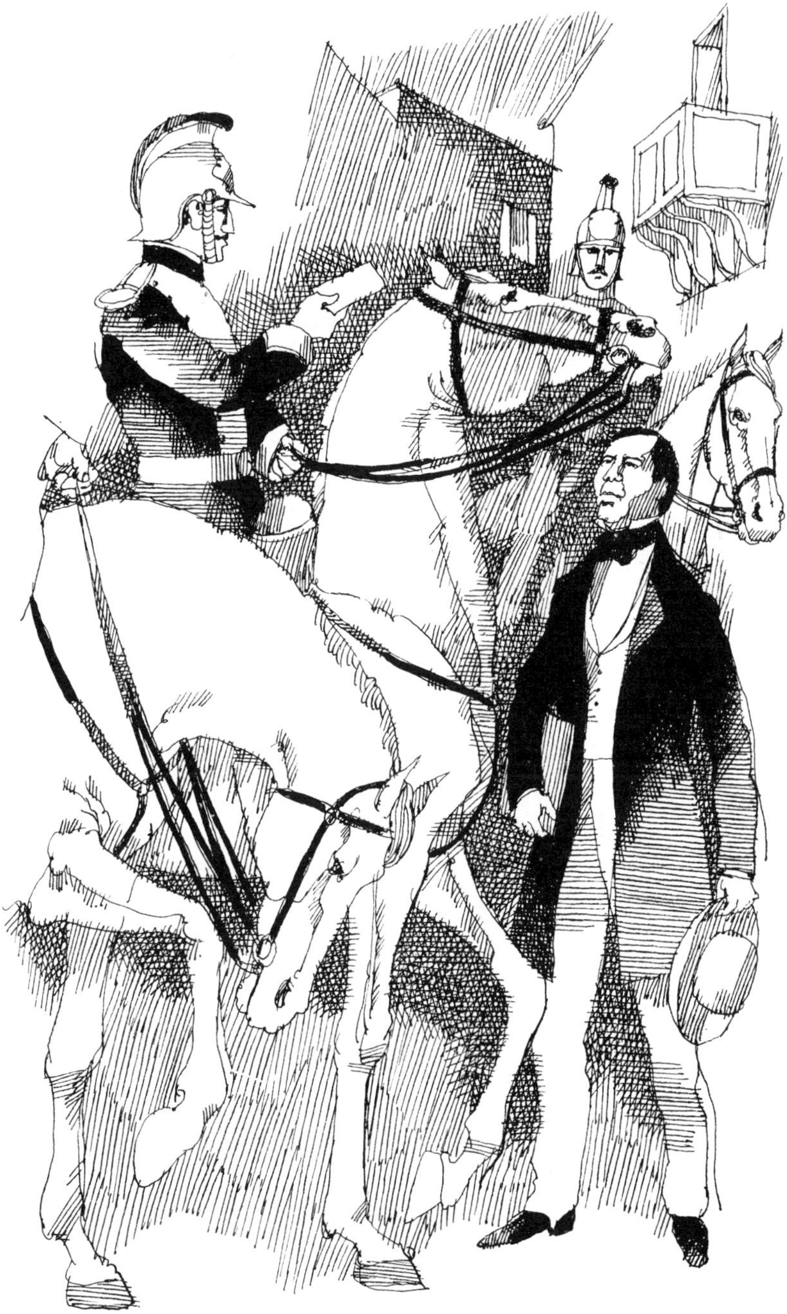

rez was escorted on foot through the streets and placed penniless aboard an English steamship about to sail for Europe.

"It would appear that some strange things happen in your country, Señor Juárez," said one of the English passengers politely. "They are things I do not approve of." This honorable man thereafter organized a collection among his fellow passengers.

The English captain was apparently of the same opinion as his passengers. When his ship reached Havana, he allowed Juárez to proceed ashore. With a few gold and silver coins in his pocket, Juárez made his way to New Orleans, a traditional place of refuge for Mexicans obliged to leave their country. There he found Melchior Ocampo, who had already been deported by Santa Anna. There, too, Juárez at last solved the mystery of his kidnapping. Until he was reminded of it, he had completely forgotten his rebuff of the fleeing general.

4 A Wandering President

Santa Anna's vengeance also overtook other Mexicans. Juárez and Ocampo were soon joined by several men who, because of their liberal beliefs, had been escorted to the frontiers of their country. Outstanding among them were Ponciano Arriaga and José-Maria Mata. Ocampo, the wealthy Creole who had traveled in Europe, was chosen as the natural leader of this group of exiles. He chose Juárez as his second in command.

All of them were almost penniless. Santa Anna

had seen to it that they were prevented from taking any cash or valuables with them. Limited sums were smuggled out of Mexico at irregular times, but during the intervals the exiles almost starved. Margarita Juárez, although she had never worked in her life, opened a little shop in Oaxaca City and sent the tiny profits to her husband. José-Maria Mata's sister managed to smuggle out a few small but valuable paintings on ivory. Arriaga once received a tiny bag of gold dust from a friend who was a miner; Ocampo obtained a couple of small emeralds.

During these hard times, Juárez reverted easily to the penury he had known as a boy. He mended frayed garments, cooked *tortillas*, and bought cheap fresh vegetables in the local market. One by one the rest of his friends obtained employment. Ocampo, remembering an interest of his student days, became a potter's assistant. José-Maria Mata found employment as a waiter. When Ocampo's daughter arrived in New Orleans to share her father's banishment, Juárez's first task was to comfort her when she wept because her bonnet was unfashionable in the American city. He then thankfully handed the housekeeping chores over to her and obtained work for himself in a printer's shop.

Juárez and his friends were content to wait. They were sure that the preposterous Santa Anna could not last. Sooner or later the Mexican people would grow weary of his greed and his high-handed ways. They would return him to the banishment he had grown to know so well. And then, perhaps, would come the turn of those whom he had so misused.

Alamán died in 1854. Santa Anna promptly organized an election along the lines that he thought it should take. Not surprisingly, he found himself again president of Mexico.

Santa Anna was confident that a peaceful term lay ahead. No enemies were in evidence. The opposition had been crushed and broken. The people were weary and longing for a period of peace in which to rebuild their disorganized lives. It was not surprising that as he felt secure from political storms, Santa Anna proceeded to live like a king.

Such splendor was costly to maintain, especially in a bankrupt country carrying a load of foreign and domestic debts, but Santa Anna soon overcame this problem. He sold to the United States a narrow strip of territory along the northern frontier, which lay to the south of the Gila River in present-day Arizona. The money was soon spent in settling some of the more pressing debts, the giving of lavish presents, and the payment of heavy graft, but it enabled his crazy regime to endure for a few more months. Santa Anna never planned for his political future; he knew he did not have one.

Meanwhile, Juárez and his companions were keeping in touch with affairs in Mexico. They knew that in the State of Guerero an old rebel leader named Juan Álvarez was preparing to revolt against Santa Anna's government. With Álvarez was a younger man named Ignacio Comonfort, who was one of the exiles' friends. He kept Ocampo well-informed about the growing strength of this latest revolutionary force.

"Send me Juárez, I pray you," Comonfort wrote in one of these dispatches. "We are short of men, powder, and money. Someone is badly needed who can organize our supplies and maintain a correspondence with our friends outside Mexico."

In July, 1854, an insignificant fishing boat crept into the splendid deepwater inlet of Acapulco. A small dark figure slipped ashore from it, unnoticed in a fisherman's costume of coarse shirt and trousers, broad-brimmed straw hat, and rope-soled sandals.

Juárez made his way through the narrow streets of the town and headed for the ugly, arid hills that lay beyond. Toward evening he reached Álvarez's camp in a shadowy mountain pass and quietly approached the lounging rebels.

"Who are you?" asked Diego Álvarez, the rebel leader's son.

"I heard that men were fighting here for freedom, so I came to give what help I can," Juárez replied.

He did not look a prepossessing rebel. His shabby clothes had been soaked by heavy rain and torn by thorns on the paths he had followed. Diego Álvarez tossed him a blanket. They gave him a plate of beans and pork. Still without announcing his identity, Juárez squatted down with the other rebels.

Several days later a messenger brought a letter to the camp. It was addressed to "The Lawyer

Don Benito Juárez." When Diego called out the name, Juárez stood up and moved forward to receive the letter.

Diego looked at him suspiciously. "You are a lawyer?" he asked.

"Yes, señor," replied Juárez.

"You are. . . . Good Heavens, you are not the Don Benito Juárez who was governor of Oaxaca?" Diego inquired hurriedly.

"Yes, señor," repeated Juárez.

"Then why in the name of the saints didn't you say so?" demanded the young man.

Juárez shrugged. "Why should I?" he asked. "What difference does it make? We are all free men and equal in this camp."

During the next few weeks, the rebels under Álvarez, Comonfort, and Juárez began to advance eastward toward the capital. Rising rebellions in other states were also threatening the existence of the central Government.

Santa Anna was able to read the signs. Over the years they had become familiar storm warnings to him. In August, 1854, he decided that the time had come for him to take another vacation outside Mexico. He departed with his usual haste and as much cash as he could collect on the way. An interim president was proclaimed, and Juárez once again was able to appear openly in the streets of Mexico City.

"Don't be fooled by the generals," he advised his friends. "They stood loyally by Santa Anna's side as long as he was master of the country. They got rid of him only when they saw that the people were turning against him—and them. No one should respect men who remember their patriotism only when they are eager to save their necks."

The temporary president resigned. A wave of popular emotion demanded that Álvarez should become his successor, but the old rebel firmly declined the honor. He nominated the younger, better-educated, and more sophisticated Ignacio Comonfort.

Ocampo was given two posts in the cabinet of Comonfort's government. Guillermo Prieto, a poet, was awarded the surprising position of Minister of Finance. Juárez, the quiet, resolute Indian, was appointed Minister of Justice and Minister of Public Education. He was then forty-nine years old.

A Wandering President

These men had already displayed, under hardship and adversity, their steadfast belief in the cause of a democratic Mexico. During their exile they had drawn up a political program, known as the Plan of Ayutla, in which they set out their convictions. They insisted that liberty must be given to the people of Mexico, that the power of the generals must be limited, and that the enormous wealth and influence of the Church must be vastly and firmly reduced.

It was an excellent plan. The proposals it contained could have changed the unhappy future history of Mexico very much for the better. Instead of remaining a primitive, feudal, and bankrupt country, Mexico might have taken her place in a world that was moving forward into an era of comparative peace and prosperity. Perhaps a nation used to governing itself and less in the habit of obeying authoritarian masters of Church and State would have welcomed and supported the Plan of Ayutla, but the Mexican people regarded it as too progressive and too much of a novelty. Comonfort, thin, shaggy-haired, stooping, a planner with an excellent brain, unfortunately was not the tough man of action that

Mexico so badly needed. He preferred to discuss the theory of politics in tranquil surroundings rather than to take any effective action that would inevitably stir up hostile feelings. The thought of a head-on collision with the Church appalled him.

Ocampo soon became disillusioned. His president was afraid to put into action the reforms that he himself had successfully introduced during the years he had been governor of Michoacán State. Although he had been born a wealthy aristocrat, Ocampo understood and sympathized with those who were trying to abolish feudal practices throughout Mexico. He resigned after two weeks in office.

"Comonfort will always bend with the wind," he said to Juárez. "I prefer to stand upright until I am borne down. I very much doubt if Comonfort, even by leaning with the wind, will be able to govern Mexico with soft words and unending patience toward those who are eager to destroy him. He is not the man to be at the head of national affairs. For the sake of Mexico, I hope I may be wrong, but I have the impression that I will be proved right."

"Whatever happens, I hope we may be given the time to destroy most of the system that has oppressed our nation for centuries," Juárez replied. "Once we have done that, the future of our own political careers should be of no importance to us."

Guillermo Prieto, the sensitive poet who was now Minister of Finance, was the next to depart. His poet's perception warned him that fresh troubles were on the way. He preferred his peaceful study and manuscripts to the dangerous world of politics.

On November 23, 1855, Juárez hammered through Congress his famous law, known as the Ley Juárez.

Defiantly he faced the rows of perturbed members, some of them openly hostile. Only here and there in that darkly somber, high-ceilinged chamber could he observe a friendly expression. José-Maria Mata was one of the few who approved. So was Ponciano Arriaga who, like Mata, had shared the humiliating discomfort of exile. With these two men was dark, hawk-faced Miguel Lerdo de Tejada, a member from the north of Mexico. Lerdo was quietly preparing his own attack on injustice and oppression. He was soon to introduce his own great law.

Hitherto, all representatives of the Church had been immune from the civil and criminal laws of Mexico. Whatever crime any priest might commit, he could never be brought to justice. The same privilege was enjoyed by the officer class of the Mexican Army. Nor was any wealthy property owner anywhere in Mexico ever brought before a court and punished for an offense. They shared the same immunity as the priests and the Army officers. But from now on, according to the Ley Juárez, all Mexicans were going to be equal in the eyes of the law.

In a country where the Church, the Army, and the wealthy privileged classes had done much as they pleased for the past three hundred years, the Ley Juárez whipped up a ferocious storm of denunciation. Violent demonstrations and fierce abuse of Juárez would have risen within the precincts of Congress Hall itself had it not been for the presence of Álvarez, the old rebel leader.

With skillful timing, he had appeared in Mexico City a couple of days earlier at the head of his Pintos, the wild half-civilized people of the re-

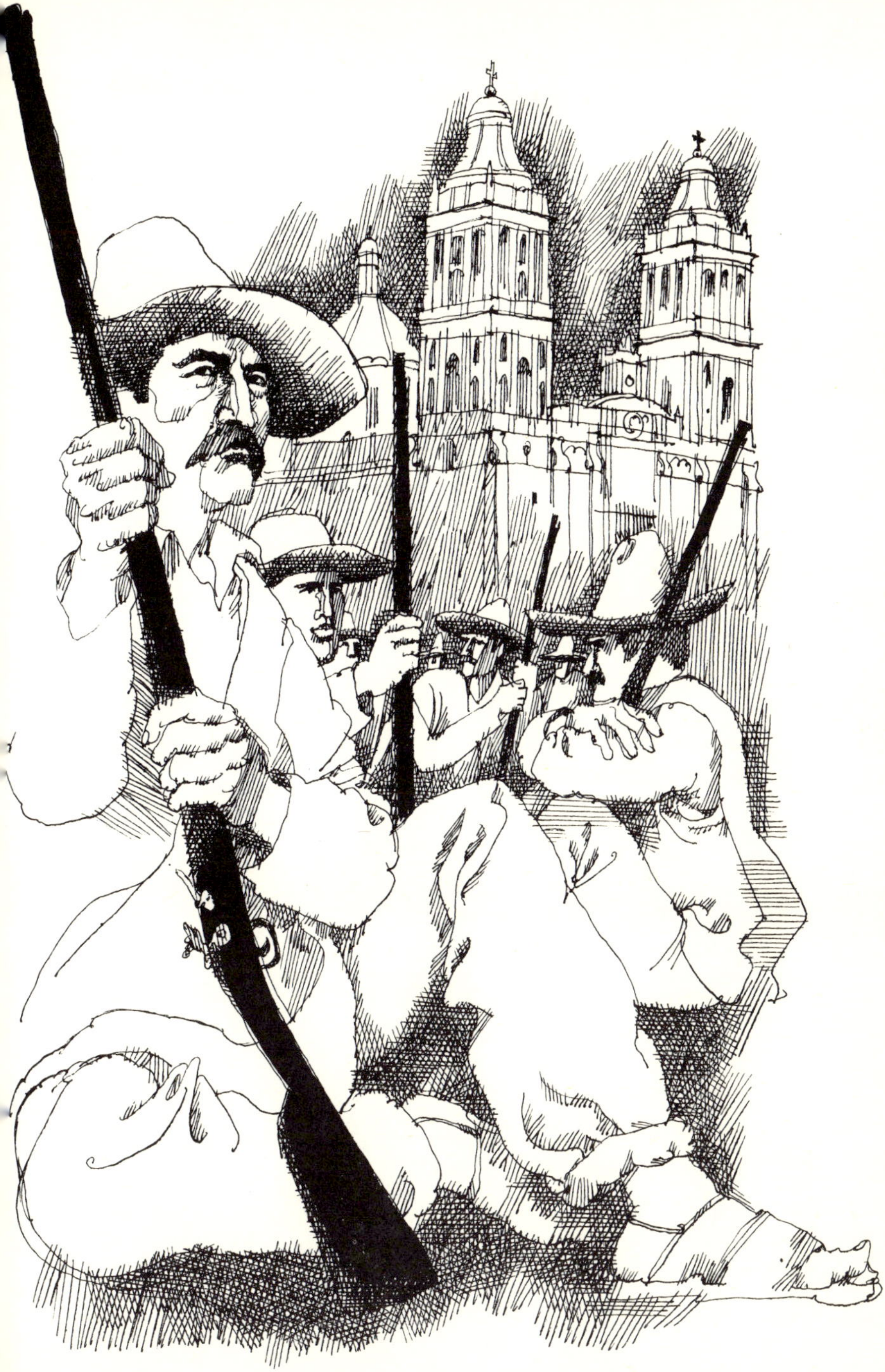

A Wandering President

mote southern regions. They were ferocious and dreaded fighters. While Juárez was speaking, three hundred of these primitive, shaggy people squatted on the plaza outside the government buildings, hugging their weapons and gazing at the passers-by in a silent, menacing way. No one cared to ask why they were there. No troops or police appeared to order them away. There they were and there they remained until Juárez had finished speaking. Comonfort retired from the chamber in dismay, and the national cabinet hastily approved the Ley Juárez by presidential decree.

While churchmen, generals, and landowners met in fury to denounce this new law, Lerdo de Tejada put the finishing touches to his own sensational piece of legislation.

On June 25, 1856, the Ley Lerdo, as it came to be known, was submitted to the Federal Government. It aroused even fiercer opposition than the Ley Juárez. Álvarez and his Pintos were no longer present on the plaza outside the Hall of Congress when Tejada rose to speak, but even the most hostile critics of the bill hesitated to start trouble in Mexico City. They knew that during the past few months the Government had reorganized the police, disciplined the senior ranks of the Army, and strengthened the power of the magistrates. The Ley Juárez was already becoming effective against malicious, would-be rioters.

The Ley Lerdo forbade the Church to own property in town or country except for buildings such as churches, schools, and others used for purely religious purposes. Such property as the Church already held—it represented enormous wealth in impoverished Mexico—could be appropriated by the Government and sold to private buyers.

The new law thus struck at the fantastic riches of the Church, which had been accumulated over the centuries by methods that were frequently questionable and too often used since independence to stir up Army mutinies or to sabotage any administration's efforts to introduce democratic measures. The leaders of the Church were able to control quite easily the entire economic and political life of Mexico. The annual income of the Church was, in fact, far greater than that of the Federal Government.

It was clear to Juárez and his earnest colleagues

that there could be no social or economic progress until this power was curtailed. Yet as they proceeded to take the necessary action, they knew they were risking the most bitter conflict their country had yet experienced. They knew also that because of the Ley Juárez the professional Army was becoming silently hostile toward their government.

Comonfort decided that the time had come to ease Juárez into a backwater where he would be removed from the sound and fury of national politics. In 1865, he was again appointed governor of Oaxaca and returned to his native state. He went with a sense of satisfaction, saying before his departure:

> At least I have achieved my ambition. I have kindled the spark that will ignite the fire of reform. That conflagration, in the years to come, will consume the rotten structure of abuses and privilege. The whole weight of public opinion adds fuel to the flames; they will not be allowed to die out.

The bishops and priests of Oaxaca naturally regarded their returned governor much as they would the Devil. They did all they could to embarrass and hinder him and refused to officiate at his inauguration, but Juárez was undaunted. He merely said:

> In that case, I shall have to manage as best I can without the prayers of the Church. It is yet another tradition that may have to be abolished. I have already done away with the guards outside the Governor's Palace because I prefer to live as a private citizen. It appears that I am gradually being freed of much of the customary tedium and supervision which my predecessors had to endure in past times.

No one ever knew for sure when Juárez was making one of his rare jests. His round, high-cheekboned face was impassive, and no gleam of humor was ever visible in his glance. Thus his jokes were seldom appreciated, particularly by those whose special privileges were his target.

Oaxaca State was still reasonably prosperous after Juárez's absence from the governorship for four years. On his return he began to teach the principle of rotation of crops, introduced new and more robust types of grain, and built fifty-four new schools throughout the state. He gave fresh encouragement to the production of exports, slowly growing in volume, that were rolling along the highway he had built to the Pacific port of Huatluco. Although the Church still frowned on him officially, a number of obscure parish priests realized the good that their governor had created throughout the state. They gave him as much assistance and cooperation as they dared. Some of them, indeed, even hinted privately that in their opinion perhaps the notorious Ley Juárez and Ley Lerdo might turn out to be good examples of sound legislation.

"Even though the Pope in Rome disapproved of your law," said one of them, "my villagers have made enough money from their crops during the past two years to pay voluntarily for repairs to my church, which has been gradually falling down for the past forty years."

In Congress, however, politics were becoming stormier than ever. The wealthy, influential classes chiefly affected by the new laws were planning to destroy the Liberal Government. In the election of 1857, nearly all the Liberal candidates lost their seats to rivals who shared Comonfort's timid views. Mexico was being edged back into the old ways. Comonfort himself was on the verge of giving way to the Church's unrelenting pressure.

Perhaps because he felt the need of a strong man at his side, Comonfort offered Juárez the post of Minister of the Interior in his new government. The position carried with it the command of the police force and responsibility for security.

It did not take Juárez long to discover that trouble was being fomented all over the country. Wealthy landowners and senior Army officers were planning revolts in several states. They were threatening, bribing, and blackmailing others to join them. The leader in all this plotting was a General Zuloaga. There was a strong movement among all these discontented men toward some violent action that would overthrow Comonfort's government and set aside the Federal Constitution of 1857, which contained the Ley Juárez and the Ley Lerdo.

As Juárez approached the President's Palace on January 21, 1858, two policemen suddenly closed in on him. He was led into a small furnished room in an obscure corner of the Palace. There he re-

A Wandering President

mained a prisoner for three weeks, being reasonably well looked after during that time but told nothing of what was going on outside.

When he was set free, he emerged to discover that the political world around him had changed. Comonfort had resigned and retired to Veracruz. General Zuloaga, a confirmed reactionary and a man of small intelligence, was now the president. He had taken over the country with 2000 troops who had supported him. His only ideas for the future of Mexico consisted of returning to the old ways and deleting the Ley Juárez and the Ley Lerdo from the Constitution.

"A remarkable position in which to find myself," said Juárez to himself as he walked out of Mexico City, almost unrecognized in the busy streets. "It is perfectly clear to me that according to law, the Minister of the Interior succeeds to the presidency should anything render the president incapable of performing his duties. I am the Minister of the Interior. Therefore, I am now the rightful president of Mexico."

Juárez was elated by the fact that the open breach had taken place at last. Now he knew where everyone stood in politics. Immediately he left for Guanajuato State to the north of Mexico City, where he knew there was strong support for the Liberals. There he openly proclaimed his presidency.

The local authorities were puzzled. They gazed speculatively at this dusty, sunburned little Indian in the big hat he had picked up somewhere along the way. He stood only five feet three inches in height, his dark suit, though travel-stained, was of good quality, his shoes, though much scratched by the rough roads, had once worn a high polish. He seemed to be penniless, yet he spoke with amazing confidence. Perhaps it might be true, thought the officials, that this really was the Don Benito Juárez who had been the highly successful governor of Oaxaca State and also the author of the famous Ley Juárez. At this stage the officials recalled that Don Juárez had until recently held the post of Minister of Justice. It might be much wiser, they decided, not to argue with him about anything; it would be more prudent to wait and see what happened. They agreed to print his proclamation on the ancient government printing press.

The officials were not kept waiting very long.

A Wandering President

Ocampo and Prieto, the distinguished poet, soon joined Juárez in Guanajuato. So did Manuel Ruiz and León Guzman, both of whom had been in the late Government. A General Parrodi appeared a few days later. With him came a mixed group of other generals and politicians. These exiles began to organize themselves at once.

Within a few weeks, a ring of states loyal to Juárez and his Liberals surrounded the Capital. On March 11, 1858, the army of General Zuloaga marched out from Mexico City, reached Guanajuato, and defeated the 7000 troops whom General Parrodi had managed to bring to Juárez's support.

Three days later a number of troops in the city of Guadalajara, where Juárez had now taken up his temporary residence, mutinied in favor of General Zuloaga. It was generally suspected that the leaders of this mutiny had been bribed by emissaries from the Church.

Juárez and his ministers were seized and cast into a locked and barred hall of the palace they were occupying. There they were left until the following morning while the fighting went on outside. Suddenly the door was flung open, and they were called upon to come out.

"These soldiers are here to kill us," someone shouted.

There was immediate panic, which Juárez quelled at once. He drew himself up, walked to the entrance of the hall, and halted as he came in sight of the leveled rifles of the mutinous soldiers.

At that moment, the poet Prieto flung himself in front of Juárez and shielded him with his body. "Put down your guns," he shouted. "Brave men are not murderers."

His gallant action so impressed the firing squad that they lowered their rifles. Their officer hesitated, then shook his head and turned aside. "I cannot give the order to fire," he muttered.

The mutiny was ended later that day upon the arrival of General Parrodi with 2000 men. The mutineers were allowed to march out of the city to join Zuloaga's victorious army.

The entire incident made so little impression on Juárez that he wrote in his diary only the following words:

> On the 13th March the Palace Guards mutinied and I was made prisoner by order of Landa, who headed the mutiny. On the 14th I recovered my liberty.

5 The Professor Becomes a General

Driven from place to place, without money, authority or a regular army, Juárez and his ministers still refused to give up the struggle. Juárez remained the rightful president by law and General Zuloaga, who had seized power for himself, was merely a usurper. The men around Juárez were aware of this fact, and so were thousands of Mexicans up and down the country. They knew that Mexico was drifting toward civil war, but no one knew how it could be averted. Better to fight such a war, thought the Liberals and their supporters, than to see Mexico plunged back into the days of Church dictatorship, shamefully inadequate elections and law courts in which the ordinary citizen had little chance of obtaining justice. The new laws of Lerdo and Juárez had provided a bright glimpse of the almost unknown world of democracy. There were many people in Mexico who were determined not to be driven back into the darkness.

After weary wanderings across Mexico, constantly moving to avoid Zuloaga's searching troops, Juárez and his fellow politicians made for Veracruz. They had decided to rally their forces at the seaport where they would stand and fight.

Veracruz had a detestable and unhealthy climate. The shoreline was low, sandy, desolate, and depressing while the city itself, damp, shabby, crumbling, smelled of dust and decaying timbers. Yet it was one of the principal ports, it could be easily defended against troops advancing on its landward side, and the population were strongly Liberal in their sympathies. They were a gruff and short-spoken people, carelessly offhand in their ways. Juárez soon found this out for himself.

He and his friends were quartered near the waterfront in a large old house. Flustered by the arrival of these strangers, their landlady paid little attention to their names. She knew vaguely that they were "important folk belonging to the Government."

Later on that first day, Juárez asked the woman for a jug of water with which to wash.

"Get it yourself," she replied. "There's a water tank down in the basement."

Juárez quietly picked up the jug and began to descend the stairs.

"Mind that you don't break that jug," the landlady screamed after him. "You'll have to pay for it if you do."

That evening the woman saw him again. Now neatly dressed, he was seated at the head of the table where he was dining with his ministers. The landlady suddenly realized who he was. She uttered a loud wail of embarrassment and fled from the room. The gentle-voiced Prieto had to be sent to persuade her to return so that the dinner could proceed.

Marching across country, ragged, thirsty and dust-covered in the blinding heat of the *tierra caliente,* detachments of soldiers began to arrive in Veracruz from the states of Coahuila, Zacatecas, Colima, and also from other parts of Mexico, to fight for the Liberal cause.

These bare-legged, penniless men, trained soldier and volunteer alike, were to form a gallant army. Poorly equipped, and with scarcely the arms to defend themselves, they had chosen to fight for the outnumbered forces of Juárez in defiance of power-hungry Zuloaga and the greedy, ambitious men around him. Matched against them was the greatly superior regular army, led by professional officers and equipped with money, arms, and supplies.

General Parrodi, who had at first supported Juárez, decided to make his peace with General Zuloaga and prudently withdrew himself from the coming fight. Juárez, forced to find a new commander-in-chief, commented bitterly that among the senior Army officers of Mexico there seemed to be a habit of trying to pick the winning team in preference to fighting on the side of justice.

Santos Degollado was the new leader chosen by Juárez. He was a plump, bespectacled college professor, who peered from behind small glasses

The Professor Becomes a General

that were generally placed crookedly on his nose. He admitted candidly that war and everything connected with it was a complete mystery to him.

Juárez was quite happy with this extraordinary man. "Degollado is just the fellow we want," he said. "Any professional officer would take fright at the poor state of our defenses and probably fly into a panic. But our Degollado will never see how bad things are. He will start from the beginning; he will piece together an army, and he will use it with his great mathematical skill."

An unorthodox theory, but it worked.

Day after day Degollado wandered round the dusty, narrow, cluttered streets of Veracruz, clutching a notebook and asking endless questions of the soldiers and officers he met. Gradually he built up a record of basic information. Men on foot could seldom cover more than twelve miles a day; the lumbering supply carts and the blazing noonday heat prevented them from covering a greater distance. Infantry should be formed into a square with fixed bayonets to resist charging cavalry. Three ranks of men, lying prone, kneeling, and standing, could deliver a simultaneous volley; they should then fall back to the rear in order to reload, and three fresh ranks should step forward to the firing point. Light muzzle-loading field guns had an effective range of about 800 yards. And so it went on.

Within a few weeks, Degollado had become a competent officer, thanks to his brilliant intellect. More than that, he began to work out troop maneuvers on a blackboard and gradually organized the disunited mass of men into Army units. He so scared the Customs officers in the port with his knowledge of figures that they almost became honest. An increased flow of money from Customs began to reach the penniless Juárez government. Degollado also had a gift for raising money, much of it from outside Mexico. He even sent José-Maria Mata to Washington in an effort to secure official American recognition for the government in exile at Veracruz.

President Buchanan's sympathies were with Juárez and his government, but he was a hard bargainer. In return for financial and material aid, he wanted to acquire for the United States the right to build a railway across the Isthmus of Tehuantepec from the Caribbean Sea to the Pacific. Mata reported the demand to Juárez:

The Professor Becomes a General

These Americans have almost a mania to seize more Mexican territory. Though I am inclined to support their idea of building this railway, I am most reluctant to see them enabled to build it by outright purchase of the Mexican soil across which the tracks must run. I think you will agree that some more acceptable alternative must be found.

While negotiations with the United States hung fire, Degollado was experimenting with his newly acquired military strategy. He marched his untried army westward, fought several indecisive actions against the Conservative forces under their twenty-six-year-old commander, General Miguel Miramón, and retired to Veracruz to make fresh notes and to study what he had learned.

Degollado came to the decision that he had, if anything, gained a slight advantage over the enemy during the summer of 1858. He was more encouraged toward the end of that same year when two of Zuloaga's generals revolted against him because of his incompetence, and Miramón immediately stepped in to depose Zuloaga. He then seized the presidency for himself. Degollado reflected that if the Conservatives kept on squabbling among themselves it would certainly help

Juárez and his legal government. Apart from everything else, Miramón's latest action would undoubtedly trouble Britain and France, both of whose governments decided to support Zuloaga's claim to the presidency. Thus encouraged, Degollado began to strengthen the wall around Veracruz with forts and then neatly worked out the firing traverse of each gun he mounted in them.

In March, 1859, President-General Miramón grandly announced that the time had come to end the civil war. He personally would provide a military demonstration as to how the Army should set about capturing Veracruz.

"I will besiege it until starvation forces Juárez to surrender," he stated. "To shorten matters, however, I may decide to shell the place into submission or else attack it with my gallant, irresistible troops."

Having arrived on the extremely hot terrain in front of Veracruz, Miramón realized that to starve a seaport city into submission, one had to have warships. What ships there were undeniably belonged to Juárez. He himself had none.

There was also a problem in connection with

The Professor Becomes a General

the plan to shell Veracruz until it surrendered. The regular army had a number of guns, but no one had remembered to supply them with sufficient shells.

Choosing his third alternative, Miramón ordered his troops to advance to the attack. Wilted by the heat, bitten by mosquitoes, and suffering from fever, the soldiers displayed some reluctance to obey. Degollado's men were safely installed behind good thick walls and opened fire enthusiastically with their well-ranged guns on Miramón's advancing forces. The latter immediately retreated, pausing only when they were well beyond range.

Not feeling secure with his other generals and all the politicians left alone while he was absent at the front, Miramón returned with his army to Mexico City. There he relieved his feelings by massacring large numbers of prisoners captured in earlier engagements. Degollado was left to contemplate the satisfactory results of his experimental defense of the city.

American warships floated at anchor in Veracruz bay during this siege. Although they remained carefully neutral, Robert McLane, the newly appointed American minister to Mexico, had closely observed the course of the unsuccessful siege from the deck of the flagship. As soon as Miramón's army had left, McLane came ashore and informed Juárez that the United States had decided to give official recognition to his government. In return for a supply of money and munitions, said McLane, Juárez's government must be prepared to cede Lower California to America. The price he suggested for that territory was twenty million dollars. On that particular issue, endless haggling was to follow for several months.

Meanwhile, the youthful Miramón was finding that being president was not altogether a happy fate. In spite of the enormous financial help given him by the Church and by Mexico's wealthiest class, his government had managed to become as bankrupt as Juárez's. In order to raise fresh funds, he had to sell off a number of state-owned properties, mostly schools and colleges, to a Swiss banking house named Jecker, Torre & Co., which had long been established in Mexico. Biting the hand that fed him, Miramón then turned on the Church, demanded a million pesos, and threat-

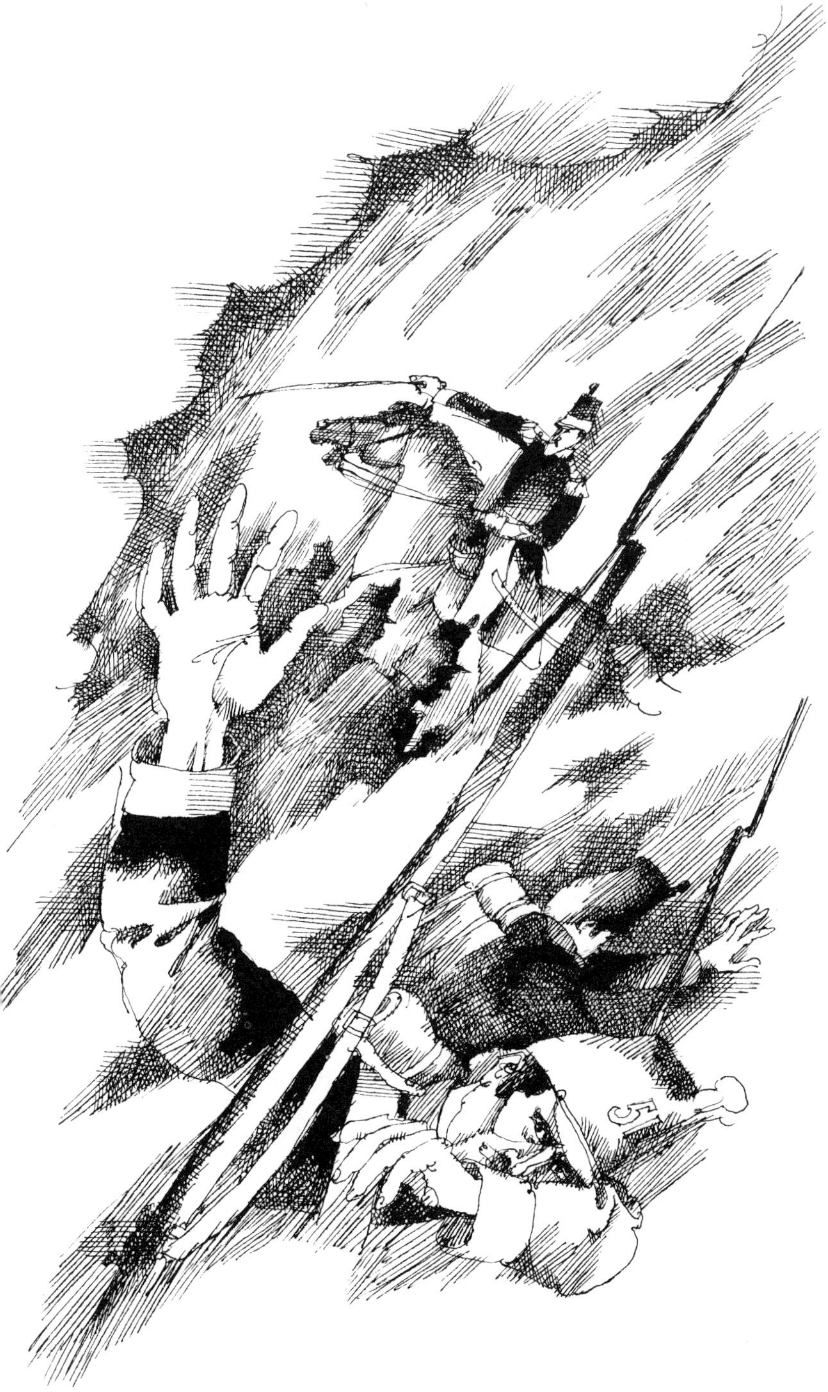

ened to sell a quantity of Church property if the money was not quickly forthcoming.

The brutal lunacy of this civil war was rapidly destroying what little economic wealth remained in Mexico.

"Though I am convinced that in the end we will win," said Juárez, "our country will be in a most desperate plight. I do not see how we are to climb out of the pit of national bankruptcy into which the whole country is rapidly sinking."

Juárez could not bring himself to agree to the sale of any Mexican territory to the United States. Only one means was left by which he could continue to finance his government's struggle against the illegal and the despotic rule of Miramón.

On July 12, 1859, one of the most important dates in Mexican history, he introduced the Reform Laws, as they were called. Based partly on the Ley Lerdo, these laws not only authorized the nationalization of Church property, but they introduced new measures that Juárez knew were essential for the progress of the nation.

They included the establishment of a civil registry for certificates of birth, marriage, and death, duties that had previously been performed exclusively by the Church, often for extortionately high fees and sometimes with injustice. The Church and the State were made entirely separate bodies so that interference by the Church in purely political matters would henceforth be illegal. In the past, public holidays had been regarded as purely religious occasions, with the Church carefully supervising the way in which the public spent its leisure time. From now on those holidays were to be observed by the people in any way they liked.

Miramón, finding himself cornered, promptly changed his mind about seizure of Church property. He suddenly announced his intention to eliminate the Ley Lerdo and the Ley Juárez from the Constitution. He followed this up by a second attack on Veracruz, which began in March, 1860, exactly a year after his first one.

"By means of a brilliant plan I have devised," he announced, "the traitor Juárez and those guilty men with him will soon be delivered into our hands."

This plan consisted of an attempt to make a seaward landing on the outskirts of the city. Miramón had obtained two small paddle steamers in

The Professor Becomes a General

Cuba, loaded them with munitions and men, and ordered them to attack.

The steamers were sighted while they were still far out to sea. They remained under observation from Veracruz while they sailed down the coast and drew nearer to the land. At that stage Juárez requested the American warships anchored in the bay to pursue and capture these mysterious intruders. An American light cruiser sailed at once and returned before dawn, bringing the two invading vessels in under her guns. Miramón's ships were later sent under American Navy escort to New Orleans, where the crews were finally released with a warning not to try such maneuvers again. The Americans sold the ships.

Miramón gave up. Once again he marched his troops back to Mexico City, while Degollado continued to work out his blackboard strategy and to devise fresh ways of raising money.

For two and a half years the war dragged on. Neither side could obtain an advantage over the other. Toward the end of 1860, the American interest in Mexico declined, owing to the threat of civil war. The limited material and financial aid Juárez had been obtaining from the United States dwindled and died away. Even Degollado could no longer devise any legal means by which fresh sums of money could be acquired for the Liberals. He could think of only one alternative:

> Our terrible need of money and absolute lack of means make me think that, in order to win a decisive battle, it would be permissible to seize 200,000 pesos from one of the *conductas* of Zacatecas that are leaving for Tampico.

These *conductas*, or mule trains, carried silver from the mines to the seaport of Tampico. The mines themselves belonged almost exclusively to British investors. Degollado was worried about the uproar Britain would create if his government helped itself to a consignment of British silver.

The idea was tried out while Degollado was still hesitating about it. An overzealous official, named Doblado, contrived to manage the affair on his own initiative, and he did it on a handsome scale, for he chose to hold up a particularly large *conducta*. Doblado excused his action saying:

> It should be easy to prove that what we have taken today is a trifling sum compared with what

the people of our country will have to pay if a war that is destroying everything is allowed to last one month longer.

The British investors took a different view. Judging by the fuss they made, they considered it most unreasonable to describe a million pesos as "a trifling sum."

Degollado, who honorably accepted all the blame for the affair, was forced to return 600,000 pesos to the British. He insisted on retaining the remaining 400,000 pesos to finance one last desperate effort to win the war. He then resigned as Minister of War and accepted a junior position on the staff of his successor, General Gonzales Ortega.

By this time the Miramón regime was in an even worse plight than Juárez and his Liberals. One of Miramón's chief officers, a scoundrel named Leonardo Marquez, broke into the British legation one night and stole 660,000 Mexican silver dollars. Apparently he had the idea of providing himself and Miramón with portable wealth when and if their flight became necessary.

It was beginning to look as if flight might indeed be necessary for both of them before long. General Ortega, a forthright and capable commander, was advancing from Veracruz on Mexico City. He had nearly reached the suburbs when, on December 22, 1860, a final battle was fought. Miramón's forces were defeated. General Zuloaga fled into the wild interior of the country, leaving his shattered army to look after itself. Miramón managed to get aboard a French warship in Veracruz, where he was able to evade the efforts of the angry British to get their hands on him for theft.

On January 11, 1861, Juárez made his ceremonial entry into Mexico City. When the day's public celebrations ended, he met privately with his elated ministers. Some were men such as Ocampo, who had remained loyally at his side since the dark days of exile in New Orleans. As always, he advised justice and tolerance:

> It is our duty, in accordance with the promises we have made, to banish all the ringleaders who sided with the usurpers against our government. I wish it were possible to display more tolerance toward them, but it is what the nation will expect. They must be exiled with tolerance and consideration and spared indignity. Enough blood has been shed in

Mexico. The time has come when we must forget what has happened in the past. We must work together to save Mexico. Our country is dangerously weak, the people are despairing. If we do not practice forgiveness and tolerance, more troubles and fresh enemies will come along and Mexico will perish. Even now I do not know if we can save the country.

NAPOLEON III

6 An Emperor's Dream

Throughout the early months of 1861, Juárez and his government tried to act swiftly to avert national disaster. Melchior Ocampo, even though he remained Juárez's faithful friend, felt unable to take part in the enormous work of reconstruction. He resigned from politics and went into retirement. He was succeeded as Minister of Foreign Affairs by Francisco Zarco, an energetic and outspoken newspaper proprietor. General Gonzales Ortega became the Minister of War.

An Emperor's Dream

Juárez was creating as strong a cabinet as Mexico could produce to face up to the chaotic financial situation.

The bank of Jecker, Torre & Co. had failed after advancing to Miramón only 1,500,000 of the 15,000,000 Mexican dollars for which he asked. Jecker had persuaded the Government of France to press his demands for the return of that money. It was a disgraceful action for France to take; men of greater integrity than the French politicians would have refused to have anything to do with the idea.

English investors were owed nearly seventy million pesos. Other European countries, including France, were owed a total of twelve million pesos.

The state of the rest of the Mexican economy provided no happier facts for Juárez and his cabinet. Agriculture had been neglected; sugarcane estates were in a disastrous plight and had failed to produce the crops world markets were eager to buy. The silver and gold mines still needed quantities of new machinery and complete modernization before they could be brought back into profitable production. Herds of cattle had decreased enormously in numbers all over the nation.

Before Lerdo de Tejada could bring his genius to the problem of nationalization of the Church's wealth, he died in February, 1861. This wealth had been estimated at one hundred and twenty-eight million pesos in 1855. During the past six years, ever since the creation of the Ley Lerdo, it had been mysteriously decreasing. The Church had given several millions to finance the war against Juárez and his Liberals, but many more millions had disappeared without trace. The financial agents of the Church, both inside and outside Mexico, had been busy during the breathing space granted them by the civil war. They had managed to conceal the Church's ownership of many valuable properties by forged documents, rigged sales, and spurious names. Great quantities of portable valuables had disappeared into secret safes and strong rooms throughout the country.

"To try to carry on the Government without money," said Juárez, "is obviously an impossibility. Yet if we dare to tell the nation the truth about our financial position, we will be blamed for something that is not our fault. It would need twenty years of peace to put Mexico on its feet again; I fear we are not going to get it."

During those months of 1861, Juárez's wiry black hair began to turn gray. New lines appeared on his face, and his friends noticed that he was beginning to walk with a slight stoop.

Juárez had other troubles besides financial ones. The new French minister, Pierre de Saligny, was a greedy, self-important little man, ambitious to make money as quickly as he could out of his new post in Mexico. He was already stirring up trouble for Juárez by turning French official opinion against Mexico. He was also busy conspiring with the men who had supported Miramón. General Zuloaga and Marquez, the robber of the British legation, were lurking in the mountains and gradually collecting a small army of cutthroats. They were already becoming a dangerous threat to the peace of the country. General Ortega, cantankerous at the best of times, was on the point of resigning from the Ministry of War. He was beginning to fancy himself as a possible successor to the presidency. Degollado had already refused to succeed him; the affair of the *conducta* still rankled him bitterly.

As news of the desperate financial plight of the nation gradually seeped out to the public, enemies began to be more boldly critical of the way that Juárez was running the country.

A fresh blow fell in June of that dismal year of 1861. Ocampo, living peacefully on his estate at Maravatio, in the state of Michoacán, was kidnapped by Marquez and murdered in the most brutal manner. Juárez noted in his diary:

> In a little while, the news spread through the city, and people of all classes came to us demanding that the political prisoners in jail be executed on the spot. They even insisted that if the Government did not do this, they and the people would do justice. I did everything in my power to dissuade these people from committing the slightest offense. As the legal ruler of society I would do everything possible to have these criminals punished according to law, but I would never tolerate violence against accused persons who were under the protection of the law and the authorities. They must bear in mind, I said, that those who sacrificed my loyal friend, Señor Ocampo, were murderers, and that I was the ruler of an enlightened society.

In his humane attitude, Juárez was at least a century ahead of his countrymen, whose ideas of

An Emperor's Dream

revenge were always powerful and apt to be lethal. Tolerance such as his was virtually unknown in distracted Mexico.

A flying column was immediately dispatched from Mexico City to track down and attack the murderers. With the troops rode Degollado, moved by a desire to clear his name. The affair was as badly managed as most of the military maneuvers. The troops were ambushed in a valley only a few miles out of Mexico City. Poorly equipped, their pay in arrears, they fled at once despite Degollado's frantic appeals to stand and fight. Degollado was shot dead as he faced the enemy alone. He was proclaimed a public hero and given a state funeral.

Encouraged by their success, Marquez, Zuloaga, and their bandits actually raided a suburb of Mexico City a few days later and were driven off only after a pitched battle in the streets. Inspired by their greed for power and profit, and a consuming lust for revenge, Zuloaga and Marquez were ready to plunge Mexico into another civil war if they could gain something from it for themselves.

Panic and hysteria spread throughout the country. Juárez's cabinet was unable to agree as to what action should be taken against the bandits. National confidence in the Government was faltering. Juárez, who believed, perhaps too strongly, in peaceful democratic measures even in the face of an emergency, was reluctant to take the strong action that the men around him demanded. To put down banditry throughout Mexico would have meant mobilizing most of the available manpower into a fresh army. This would have caused enormous strain on the already bankrupt treasury; it might even plunge Mexico into utter ruin.

The Minister of Foreign Affairs, Francisco Zarco, wrote about it in his newspaper:

> To defeat these ruthless and vicious outcasts from society is not a task that would be long or arduous. It is a matter of seven million men defending themselves against two thousand murderers. One week of the harshest measures will save the situation.

With his own government turning against him, Juárez could do no more. On July 17, 1861, he took the only possible course of action that remained open to him: leaving Marquez alone, he declared the suspension for at least two years of interest payments on the foreign national debt.

It immediately became clear to the outside world that Mexico was on the verge of bankruptcy. France at once broke off relations with Mexico. The British, acting more cautiously, only suspended relations. Spain did the same. Now Mexico was cut off, powerless and utterly alone.

The leading statesmen of France, England, and Spain met in solemn conference to decide what should be done about Mexico. In spite of their polite diplomatic language, these powerful spokesmen were in a touchy mood.

Spain naturally took a deep and emotional interest in the affairs of a country that had been a romantic part of her vanished colonial empire. She was no longer powerful enough to attempt single-handed the task of restoring a stable government in Mexico. In any event, there was no reason why she should; Spain got nothing from Mexico and Mexico got nothing from Spain.

The diplomatic representative of France was aware of the thousands of French investors who were clamoring for repayment of the money they thought they were in danger of losing in Mexico.

He was also aware that the Emperor of France, Napoleon the Third, was dreaming up some extraordinary plan for Mexico that might brighten his record as a monarch. But France was reluctant to put herself to the vast expense that would be necessary to restore peace and stability.

The English diplomats were conscious that their own country was owed the most money by Mexico, seventy million pesos. They could congratulate themselves on the fact that even in money matters the British investors believed in displaying a certain amount of restraint. They were making a great deal less noise about Mexico than the French. Moreover, Britain had the largest and most effective Navy and was the most wealthy of the three nations concerned. The English were prepared to go along with the French and Spanish, but insisted that the going should be on their terms and no one else's. The British Government was inclined to believe that recently the French had been badly misled as to conditions in Mexico, thanks to the misinformation supplied them by the scheming Saligny.

While the statesmen of these three countries continued their lengthy discussions, the French

An Emperor's Dream

Emperor, Louis Napoleon, was busy with his own pet scheme to make Mexico a monarchy and to put Prince Maximilian of Austria on the throne.

Napoleon had secretly admired and envied Maximilian since they had first met some five years earlier. Tall, blond, blue-eyed, and good-looking, the thirty-year-old Maximilian came of one of the most ancient and distinguished families in Europe, the Hapsburgs. He had charming manners and the superb self-confidence of a born aristocrat. Four years before he had married the Archduchess Charlotte, the young and lovely daughter of Leopold, King of the Belgians. The young couple were idyllically happy and preferred to spend most of their time together in their little Castle Miramar on the rocky and picturesque shores of the Adriatic. They led a gay, cultivated life, had numerous friends, and were generally in debt.

Maximilian had no chance of ever becoming emperor of Austria. It was most unlikely that Charlotte would ever become queen of the Belgians. Yet they would make a distinguished couple, thought Napoleon, to sit on any throne, particularly the throne of Mexico. With Maximilian installed as emperor through French efforts, the links between France and Mexico would be strengthened; a profitable trade could be developed between the two countries, and expansion or interference by America would be firmly checked. Finally he, Napoleon, would receive much credit from the French nation for having created the entire plan. At last he would have proved to the world that he *was* a worthy successor of the great Napoleon Bonaparte.

When first approached by Napoleon's emissaries with this daring scheme, Maximilian was not enthusiastic. He regarded Napoleon as a very ordinary little man "who felt uncomfortable in the presence of a prince of more ancient family than his own." While the idea of being an emperor in his own right appealed to Maximilian, and much more so to the Archduchess Charlotte, he wanted to be sure that he would be maintained on that throne by an armed force that was more reliable than the Mexican Army. Until he was sure that Napoleon's scheme would secure the support of the other major powers, Maximilian preferred to wait before making a decision.

While France, Spain, and England began to

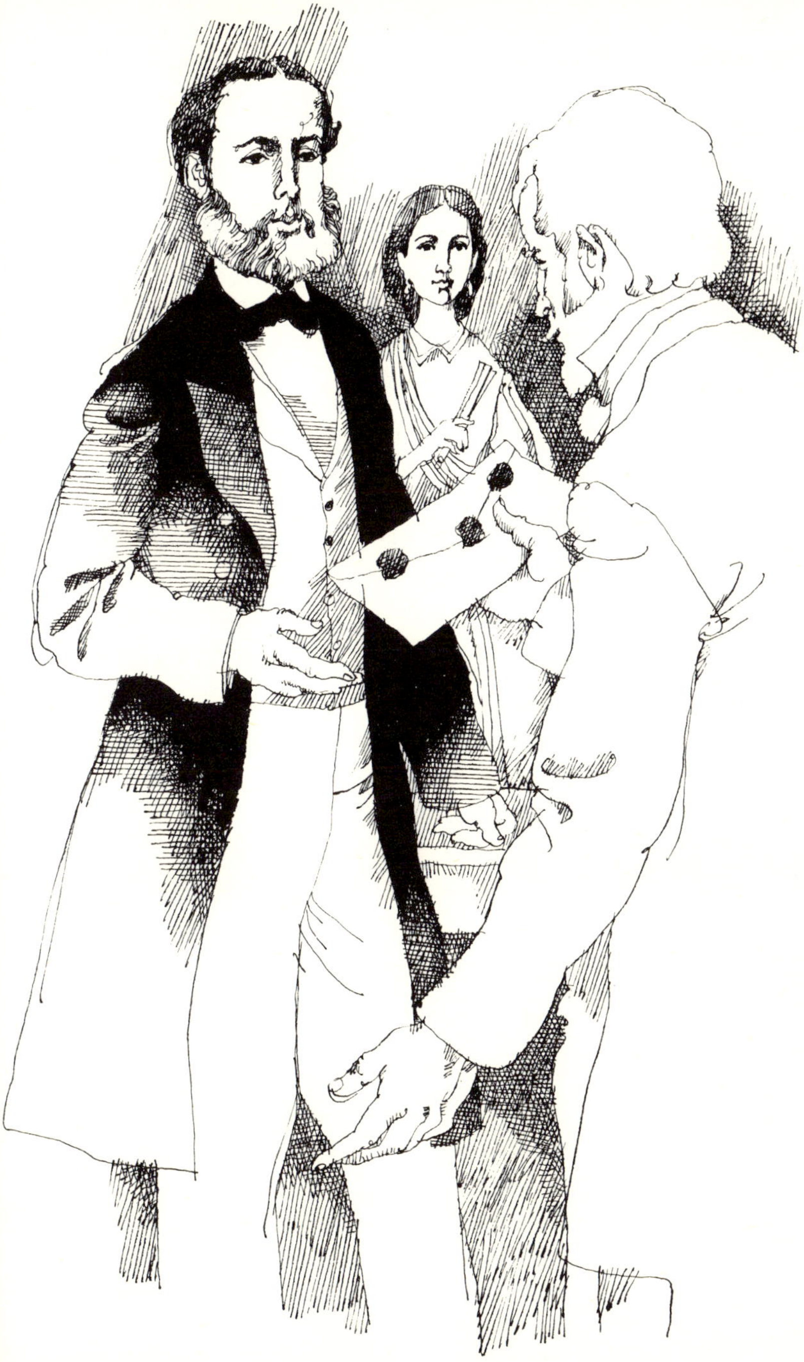

discuss the sending of an expeditionary force to Mexico, Juárez was still struggling to restore order. General Ortega was sent with a strong military expedition to deal with Marquez and dispersed the outlaws after a hard-fought battle. The French creditors were approached and offered security in the form of confiscated Church property. They were inclined to accept this offer until the French minister, Saligny, advised them not to do so. Saligny feared that the democratic government that Juárez was trying to introduce would interfere with the many little moneymaking schemes, most of them illegal, in which he was engaged on the side. He favored a government comprised of industrialists, Army generals, and crooked politicians, all of whom would be so busy amassing wealth for themselves that they would leave him alone to continue accumulating his own. Saligny was quite prepared to place his own interests before those of his country.

The English minister to Mexico, Sir Charles Wyke, was an elderly bachelor, a former Army officer, who enjoyed his own large private income. He had little sympathy with Juárez, or with Mexico generally, for he regarded most of the country's troubles as the fault of the Mexicans themselves. He was largely right, but his loud and frequent expression of these views to Juárez and the Cabinet scarcely made him a popular figure among them. Their only relief was provided on the occasions when Sir Charles chose to pick on Saligny instead.

The United States was fortunate in her minister to Mexico. The Lincoln administration appointed Thomas Corwin, an old friend and supporter of Mexico. This appointment greatly alarmed the Confederates. One Southern newspaper declared:

> Corwin is a man who more than any other can attract the sympathies of Mexico. His appointment will have a great influence on the efforts that are being made to prevent us from being recognized as a nation.

Corwin advised his government to guarantee the interest on the Mexican foreign debt for five years, informing them:

> I am sure that Mexico would be willing to pledge all her public lands and mineral rights in Lower Cali-

fornia, Chihuahua, Sonora, and Sinaloa, for the payment of this guarantee. . . . I cannot find in this Republic any men of any party better qualified, in my judgment, for the task than those in power at present.

The Lincoln administration approved of Corwin's idea. Sir Charles Wyke became alarmed lest the United States gain a lead over England in Mexican affairs. He proposed alternative forms of assistance to Juárez. It was as if two doctors stood haggling while an untended patient was bleeding to death. Before Juárez could reach any final decision, the London Convention was signed by France, Spain, and England on October 31, 1861. This pact agreed on an expedition to occupy the ports and military strongholds of Mexico. The Mexican Customs were to be placed under their joint control, and the three countries hoped to regain the sums owed to them from the duties they collected. Mexico would just have to get along without this valuable revenue. At the same time, the powers pledged themselves not to seize any Mexican territory nor to interfere with the rights of the Mexican people to choose their own government. Meanwhile, in his charming little castle beside the sea, Maximilian continued to hesitate before giving a final decision. He was an intelligent young man with considerable political experience, and he had views of his own on the subject of Mexico:

> Up to the present the plan for my accession to the throne of Mexico has only been discussed in Europe. Before I reach a decision, I must wait to see how the Mexican people themselves react to the plan. I do not think they will be very enthusiastic, and in that case my throne would rest on shaky foundations that might crumble at any time.

On December 8, 1861, expeditionary vessels from Spain reached Veracruz. Six days later the town was formally occupied by 6000 Spanish troops.

The unpredictable nature of the Mexicans now began to reveal itself. On instructions from Juárez, whom he somewhat opposed, the governor surrendered the town. It was entirely the governor's own idea to retreat into the interior, where he immediately began to organize guerrilla bands to harass the invaders. This was not at all what Admiral Rubicalva, the commander of the Spanish expedition, had expected. He had read the dispatches from Monsieur Saligny in which that rapacious man had stated that as soon as foreign troops landed, the Mexican Government would collapse. Most of the politicians would side with Britain and France, and Juárez would take to flight. So probably, added Saligny, would General Ortega, now the vice-president, and also Ignacio Zaragoza, the young veteran soldier who had recently become Minister of War.

But on finding themselves invaded by foreign powers, the Mexican people actually began to think with affection of "the little Indian," as they called Juárez. Without money, short of arms and munitions, they rallied to defend the government that, only a few weeks earlier, they had been busily criticizing. Their first defiant volleys from the inland hills sent Admiral Rubicalva and his Spanish troops scampering back into Veracruz.

In Mexico it had always been the custom to find new recruits for the Army by sending out parties of veteran soldiers under an officer to seize any likely young men they met in the fields or villages. These men were marched back to the nearest barracks. Care had to be taken to insure that they did not make a run for liberty on the way. Once enlisted in the Army, the recruits risked a sentence of death if they attempted to desert. Most of them preferred to remain until their term of three years' service came to an end.

In December of the year 1861, there was no need for the Army to secure recruits by the usual press-gang methods. All over the country, thousands of young men lined up to volunteer their services. By the time the English and French fleets reached Veracruz early in January, Juárez knew that his countrymen had decided to fight. The only problems were how to feed, clothe, and arm this new and ever-growing army in Mexico. Payment of the troops was an impossibility; the national treasury was practically empty.

Juárez remained calm in the face of this latest infliction and announced:

> The Mexican Government is prepared to discuss every legitimate claim upon it. In the meantime we do not intend to declare war but only to repel force by force. Let us defend ourselves against the hostile invasion to which our country is being now submitted by strictly observing the laws and customs of humanity. The enemies of Mexico have described

An Emperor's Dream

us to the world as an uncultivated and degraded people. By our conduct toward these invaders let us prove that we are a people worthy of the liberty and independence left us by our forefathers.

Meanwhile, the allies were running into their first troubles at Veracruz. The Spanish had landed 6000 troops, the French 5000, and the British 700 marines. The French and Spanish leaders had received orders from their governments to march into the interior of the country. The English troops, however, were under orders to remain in Veracruz, for the British were familiar with the risks and dangers of trying to fight a campaign in an unhealthy tropical country. They had learned the hard facts in the many battles fought in Africa, India, and the Far East. Veracruz was a most unhealthy spot, where the troops were bound to suffer casualties from fever, but the interior of Mexico would be certainly even more unhealthy for them.

The arrival of 6000 more Spanish troops in Veracruz made it essential for the planned march to begin. The port was hopelessly overcrowded, the wharves were jammed with military stores that were already rotting in the blazing heat of the sun. Five hundred Spanish troops were down with fever and numbers of French troops were beginning to sicken. The English suffered less. The hygiene of their camp was excellent, their food was of a better quality, and care was taken to protect it against the myriads of flies. The tents and rooms in which they slept were equipped with insect screens.

The French and Spanish began their march into the interior. The English marines followed them four or five miles out of Veracruz and then returned to the town. Juárez, with remarkable restraint, allowed the march to be made in peace. Having endured the climate of Veracruz, he knew what an ordeal the troops must be experiencing.

The allied force went only twelve miles inland before its leaders realized that their lack of wagons and mules—which they had completely overlooked bringing with them to Mexico—made it impossible to go any further from the coast. At the village of La Terjeria they made camp while senior military officers and diplomats continued to squabble among themselves in the unpleasant heat of Veracruz.

An Emperor's Dream

Saligny had advised his government to insist on the repayment of the 1,500,000 Mexican dollars the banking house of Jecker, Torre & Co. had advanced to Miramón's government. The French had continued to press for settlement of this claim, along with the twelve million pesos they were already owed.

The English diplomats were now concerned over the fact that the French were beginning to show an inclination to take over Mexico for themselves and run it their own way. They were still more upset when Miramón, who had been an accomplice in the theft of 660,000 Mexican dollars from the safe of the British legation in Mexico, arrived in Mexico and appeared to be on friendly terms with the French. Finally the British were outraged by the French demand for Mexico's repayment of the Jecker bonds.

The Spanish sided with the English. The costs of their expedition were proving ruinous to an already impoverished Spain, and their numbers of sick were increasing every day. They were beginning to see that by the time the French had seized all they could lay their hands on, there would be little left for anyone else.

The alliance disintegrated. England and Spain made peace with Juárez and began to withdraw their forces from Mexico in April, 1862. France promptly responded by bringing several thousand fresh troops to Veracruz.

Juárez realized that his country was now facing a determined enemy, bent on the destruction of the democratic system he had spent so many years trying to introduce. Bankrupt though Mexico was, ill-armed and entirely without allies, he still would not yield. As long as the nation remained loyal, he would continue to fight the invader. On April 12, 1862, he declared war on France.

7 The French Invaders

A disapproving Europe gradually learned what France was trying to do in Mexico. The English people had not sympathized with the idea of the expedition and were deeply thankful that their troops had been recalled. As one national newspaper put it:

> What had Britain to do with all this? Nothing; absolutely nothing. She served merely to accompany the burglars to the door and to stand there as a lookout while the crime was committed.

The French people did not know what to make of the whole situation. No one could blame them. They had been told that their army was proceeding to Mexico with the English and Spanish to reestablish law and order and to secure repayment of Mexico's debt. England and Spain had then pulled out of the expedition. Now France was at war with Mexico, and there seemed to be some discussion about placing that handsome young man, Prince Maximilian of Austria, on the throne of Mexico and thus turning him into a kind of emperor. In the meantime, the matter of Mexico's national debt seemed far from settled. It was all very perplexing.

In Mexico, the French General de Lorencez was also becoming confused. With 8000 seasoned troops under his command, it seemed impossible that the ill-disciplined and badly armed Mexicans could offer any serious resistance. Yet as he began his march inland toward Mexico City, those dusty, ragged men in the big hats began to fight more seriously than he had dreamed possible. It was not what Saligny, the supposed expert on Mexican affairs, had predicted.

A hundred miles inland from the coast, where

The French Invaders

the road climbed upward through steep gorges to a vast plateau, Zaragoza, the young commander-in-chief appointed by Juárez, held up the French advance for three hours and inflicted a number of casualties on them.

It was here that for the first time Lorencez began to regret the hasty dispatch he had sent to the French Minister of War:

> We are so superior to the Mexicans in race, in organization, in discipline, in morality that I beg Your Excellency to be so good as to inform the Emperor that, at the head of eight thousand soldiers, I am already master of Mexico.

The deeper the French went into Mexico, the more bitter the fighting became. Every town, hillside, cliff, and fort seemed to contain Mexicans who were fighting with a ferocity the bewildered French had never expected. At the Cerro de Guadalupe, a steep hill with a fort and convent on top 140 miles inland from the coast, Lorencez lost 462 men killed, wounded, or missing. His nerve was broken, and Saligny got drunk in despair. Back to France went a hasty dispatch requesting 20,000 reinforcements and some heavy guns. Lorencez then retreated to Orizaba to await the arrival of the men and supplies. It was the end of him in Mexico. He was soon replaced by a new officer, General Frédéric Forey.

Juárez continued to control his government and direct the war from the Presidential Palace in Mexico City. To a distinguished Frenchman in Paris, who suspected that the war had been a mistake from the beginning, he wrote:

> There is a deliberate intention on the part of the [French] Imperial Government to humiliate Mexico and impose its will upon us. This is a truth confirmed by facts; there is no help but defense. The arrival of new and numerous troops has caused us no fear or discouragement; on the contrary it has revived public spirit, and today there is but one sentiment in the whole country, the defense of the liberty and independence of Mexico. . . . The Imperial Government will not obtain the submission of the Mexicans, and its armies will not have a single day of rest.

By March, 1863, nearly 30,000 French troops were in Mexico. During the winter on the high plateaus they almost froze to death. In summer they fainted or fell exhausted by the roadside in

The French Invaders

the intense heat. Their bodies were racked by the *vomito* sickness, a severe type of fever that often proved fatal. The countryside swarmed with snakes and venomous insects. Day and night, muskets cracked on nearby hillsides, and from the shadow of deep rocks, Mexican bullets whined through the ranks of the French. A double hurricane struck their fleet anchored at Veracruz, sinking eight warships and five merchant vessels, drowning hundreds of troops and sailors.

While the French newspapers were busily calming the increasing doubts and fears of their readers, the splendid French army with their field guns, their mule trains, their smart red-and-blue uniforms, and their improved Minie rifles, continued a painfully slow advance toward Mexico City. One thought kept driving officers and men: American troops had fought their way into the capital in 1847. What had been done once could be done again. Any withdrawal now would be taken by the world as a sign that French troops were incapable of repeating a military feat that the Americans had accomplished sixteen years earlier.

As the French drew nearer to the capital Juárez

knew that his government must retreat. Mexico City could not be defended without causing great casualties among the civilian population. As the flag outside his Palace was lowered at sunset on the evening of May 31, 1863, Juárez appeared near the base of the white flagstaff to acknowledge the greetings and cheers of the vast crowds that had gathered. A band struck up the national anthem and a company of troops presented arms. For a few moments Juárez remained at attention. As the flag fluttered down, he stepped forward and stooped to kiss the folds. Then raising his head he called in his loud, clear voice, "*Viva Mexico!*" The crowd responded with a crashing cheer, and Juárez quietly passed into the entrance and out of sight. Darkness fell, the throngs of people slowly dispersed, and lights began to appear in the streets. The windows of the Palace, however, remained in darkness that night.

Juárez and his government were already on their way out of the city to carry on the resistance from the state capital of San Luis Potosí.

On June 7, 1863, General Forey and his troops marched into the city. General Forey, never un-

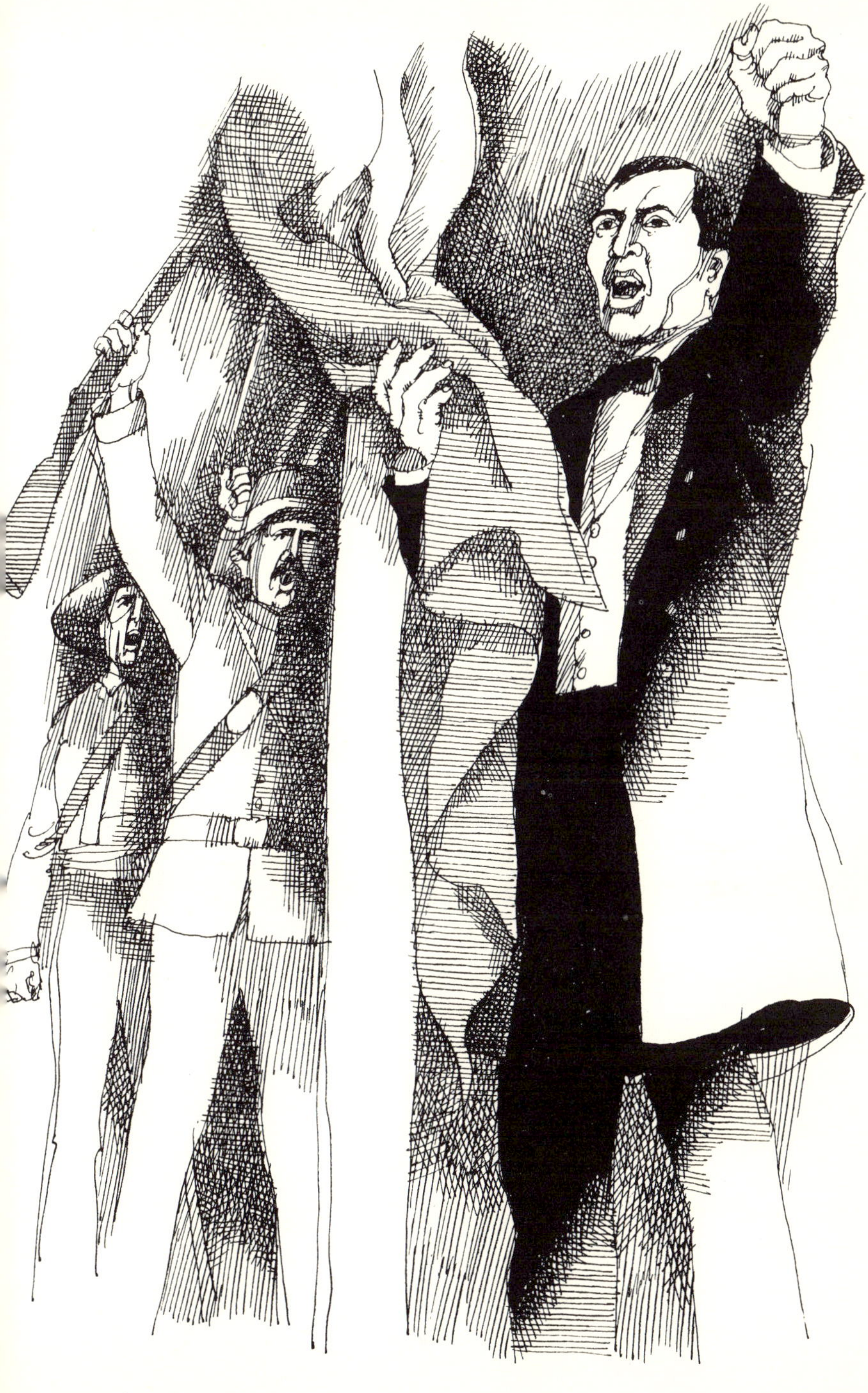

The French Invaders

derstood the Mexican people. A vain and obstinate man, he invariably insisted on placing his own interpretation on facts.

On June 12, General Forey proceeded to infuriate the democratically inclined Mexicans, a majority of the people. He announced that religion would be respected, Church property would be left alone, the press would be free but controlled. The bishops would be recalled, and the Mexican Army "reorganized," which meant that every officer suspected of remaining loyal to Juárez would be discharged.

The General then proceeded to select an Assembly. There were thirty-five members, carefully chosen by Forey himself, all of the Conservative party. They were almost compelled to accept the positions for fear of offending the French, but they were frightened and worried men. None of them could forget that only two hundred miles to the north, the "small dark Indian" was still the leader of a properly elected Government of Mexico. They themselves would be regarded at the best as puppets and at the worst as traitors.

"Poor devils," wrote an observant French officer who attended the opening of the Assembly, "their faces, manners, and costumes by no means corresponded to what we then thought the representatives of a people should be."

There was another reason why the Assembly members were frightened out of their wits. They had been given strict instructions by Forey to vote for a monarchy in Mexico, and they lacked the courage to refuse. But if the day ever came when they found themselves trying to explain to Juárez and the Mexican people why they had taken this step, they might well end up by wishing themselves dead.

Beside the peaceful Adriatic coast, Maximilian was displaying an obstinate spirit, insisting:

> If I am to accept the throne of Mexico, then it must be with the consent of the Mexican people. And once I am on the throne, I will need the cooperation of France to ensure that I remain there.

The vote of the puppet Mexican Assembly was transmitted to him over the telegraph wires as expressing the wish of the nation. The presence of 30,000 French troops in Mexico City seemed a sound guarantee that the throne would be se-

The French Invaders

curely maintained. Although the young Archduchess Charlotte was growing more eager and excited every day at the prospect of being the empress of Mexico, Maximilian still remained doubtful. He knew that the Mexicans were an emotional people with an unstable political history. Compared with the cultivated circles and sophisticated European society in which he and Charlotte lived, Mexico City was on the edge of the jungle. Some intuition kept warning him that by accepting the throne he might expose his wife and himself to more than disappointment.

News of the French entry into Mexico City gave Maximilian much encouragement. Napoleon kept urging him to accept the Mexican offer, and the Emperor Franz Joseph was at last becoming slightly enthusiastic at the idea.

In July, 1863, Maximilian finally gave his reluctant consent. It had taken him nearly three years to decide. "If I heard the whole thing was called off," he said privately to a friend, "I assure you I would dance for joy. I dislike the way I've been coaxed, tempted, and persuaded into undertaking this business."

Maximilian and Charlotte reached Mexico City

in June, 1864. They were given an impressive public welcome, the streets were full of banners and smartly uniformed French troops, and there was much cheering from the crowds who lined the sidewalks. But already mutters of warning thunder were rumbling in the distance.

The United States Congress passed a sharply worded condemnation of the French plans for the creation of a Mexican throne. The English suddenly became very cool and noncommittal. Spain, too, withdrew and refused to take an active part. A young French officer who was gifted with rare insight into Mexican national affairs had already expressed his doubts in a letter to France:

> What a sorry task we shall give poor Maximilian and what a disillusionment we are preparing for him. When he lands at Veracruz and sees that his whole empire consists of the road to Mexico City, a road on which he will have to be heavily escorted not to be carried off, and when he finds in his capital neither finances, nor justice, nor army, but organized pillage and the parties squabbling and tearing one another apart, to what saint will he turn...? Naturally he will fling himself into the arms of Monsieur de Saligny, Marquez, the Church, and the landowners, and then everything will be completely lost.

The French Invaders

France will exhaust her army and her treasure without succeeding in seating Maximilian on his throne.

In earlier letters, this same officer, Captain Loizillon, had expressed his shrewd opinion on many other aspects of Mexican affairs and supplied some interesting information regarding the various little schemes that Monsieur Saligny was operating.

These letters subsequently came to the attention of Napoleon. For the first time in his rosy dreams of Mexico, the cold fingers of reality chilled his optimism. General Forey was hurriedly recalled. So was the odious Saligny. General Bazaine, Forey's second-in-command, shrewder and a more capable officer, was placed in supreme command. While Forey sulked, and Saligny wept, Bazaine grimly read the private instructions given him by the now worried Napoleon.

> You will try to repair the unfortunate mistakes that have been made since the entrance of the army into Mexico City.... The election of the Archduke Maximilian must be endorsed by the greatest possible number of Mexicans. The hasty nomination that has been made is not regarded in Europe as a just

expression of the will of the country.... You must see to it that the new Government of Mexico does not unjustly favor the Church, the wealthy classes, or those who rigidly supported the Conservative Governments of past years.

Maximilian and Charlotte were doing their honest best to win the respect and affection of the Mexican people. They were learning Spanish, wore the national costume, and carefully attended all public ceremonies, where they mixed freely with the crowds. By their charm and good manners they had already made a great many Mexican friends. But Maximilian was still not comfortable; he continued to be haunted by a strange feeling of insecurity, which even the obvious happiness of his wife could not disperse. Like the timid members of the puppet Assembly, he was obsessed by thoughts of the "small, dark Indian." At last he wrote to Juárez, suggesting that they should meet in order to discuss the present situation and try to work out a peaceful understanding for the future. The cold but courteous reply that Maximilian received from San Luis Potosí only increased his misgivings.

Juárez, writing "as President of the Republic,"

refused to come to Mexico City for the proposed meeting. In chilly, carefully weighed words he pointed out the falsity of Maximilian's position as emperor of Mexico:

> You employ men like Marquez, and you surround yourself with all that condemned part of Mexican society. Frankly, I have suffered a disappointment: I thought you one of those pure beings whom ambition could not corrupt.

Maximilian could not fail to sense Juárez's bitter determination never to yield to France's ambitions and plots in Mexico. The struggle must continue between them for mastery. As far as Maximilian knew in those despairing days that followed his reading of the letter, the only brightness was provided by the remarkable success that General Bazaine was having. This officer was proving that he was also a first-class civil administrator and a competent diplomat. He was, indeed, the only Frenchman who proved himself a worthwhile rival to Juárez in his understanding of the Mexican people.

Bazaine refused to allow the new Government to seize the property of those who remained loyal to Juárez. The Archbishop of Mexico, who had recently returned, was put firmly in his place when he started the first of his customary intrigues. Smooth-tongued politicians out for promotion and profit found themselves scared and silent when Bazaine's cold blue eyes were turned in their direction. His Mexican army, far from being disbanded, found itself receiving good rations, regular pay, and unusual consideration from the authorities. Not unnaturally, the quality and morale of the troops began to improve.

In well-planned military moves, Bazaine captured one city after another from the scanty, ill-provided garrisons that still held out. Querétaro fell into the hands of the French, followed by Guanajuato and the pleasant town of Guadalajara. Bazaine knew, however, that even with 30,000 troops in the country, he had not enough to quell all Mexico.

In San Luis Potosí, Juárez grew uneasy. Seated behind his desk in the Governor's Palace, he received daily the reports and messengers that reached him from all over Mexico. The information all pointed in one general direction: his government was gradually falling to pieces as more

The French Invaders

and more of his former supporters made their peace with the French. Scattered units of his troops were still fighting, backed up by many thousands of guerrillas, but with every day that passed it became more difficult for them to hold back the solid advances of the French regiments. For the first time in their married life, even Margarita became apprehensive for the future. She proposed to Juárez that they should move northward to Monterrey in the State of Nuevo León where they would be close to sanctuary across the American border, but he was unwilling.

> I shall retreat when I have to but I shall never leave the soil of Mexico. As long as I remain here, the French and their puppet Congress can never claim to be the rightful Government of the country. Meanwhile, the more thinly we can spread the French over Mexico, the greater will their casualties be and the heavier their expenses. The people of France are already grumbling about the ever-rising costs of their expedition to Mexico. Between their horror of unnecessary extravagance and the climate of northern Mexico, we will beat them yet. By all means let French troops continue to pursue me across the unpleasant deserts; it will speed their disillusionment with the Mexican venture.

Juárez was right. The French nation was gradually realizing that their emperor was fighting for the success of his own scheme in Mexico. As the small investors were slowly repaid the money they were owed, they became more and more determined to have nothing further to do with Mexico. Their attitude began to affect the whole of France.

"We are erecting a Government in Mexico," suggested one of the national newspapers, "which will collapse immediately when our troops withdraw."

A wittily sharp-tongued journalist expressed his convictions in a remark that was soon circulating throughout France. "To my mind," he declared, "Napoleon will break his neck in Mexico if he is not hanged beforehand."

The French military columns came northward after Juárez. In December, 1864, he was forced to leave San Luis Potosí with the remnants of his government, and to make for Nuevo León. On the day after his arrival at the Governor's Palace in that state, he wrote to his wife, who had decided to remain for a few days with friends in a nearby town:

At ten o'clock today I made my entrance into the city. I did not do so yesterday because this Señor Governor (who has been a little too friendly toward the French) is very fond of talebearers. He believed that we were coming to attack him and had made preparations for defense, taking possession of the artillery in the citadel and spreading word that no help was to be given to the Government. All this is nothing but bluster and clowning, but I do not let on that I understand. . . . Pick up the clothes brush which I left on my shaving table. Regards to our friends and many hugs for the children.

Your husband,
Juárez.

The stay in Nuevo León was short. Early in 1865, Juárez was forced to move north again, this time to Chihuahua. Far to the south of him, in odd corners of Mexico, on windswept hillsides, and in dark ravines, the incredible Mexican fighters who still remained loyal to Juárez and his government continued to lurk like aggressive scorpions. Even General Ortega, that vain, temperamental but successful soldier, was still continuing the fight. His army now consisted of only 2000 men, and they were forced to follow the strategy of the local civilian guerrillas.

The outlook for Juárez appeared bleak, but his obstinate courage remained unshaken, and he declared:

> Forty-five thousand French troops in the country now. An extra fifteen thousand men for France to pay and feed. No wonder the French are grumbling more loudly about the expense of this war. I hear that Maximilian has begun to squabble with the Church. I think that before long, my friends, our tide will begin to turn. We will be in Mexico City again one of these days.

JUÁREZ

8 An Endangered Throne

Maximilian was indeed beginning to have his troubles. Despite public loans made in France to bolster up his Mexican throne—loans based on highly colored stories of the natural mineral wealth of the country—his administration was running short of funds. A proportion of the Customs duties was being handed over to the Government by the French authorities, but the sums were simply not sufficient to keep the country going. The bishops advised all those tenants living in premises that had once belonged to the Church to pay no more rents to the Government. This was another severe blow to the national finances.

There was also the constant worry over the steadfast refusal of the United States Government to recognize Maximilian as emperor of Mexico. In his message to Congress of December, 1865, President Johnson, who had succeeded Lincoln, spoke disapprovingly of the presence of French troops in Mexico and declared that it must cause friction between France and the United States as long as it continued.

The constant strain on Maximilian provoked him into an action that in more normal times he would have refused angrily to consider. He outlawed all those Mexicans, both soldiers and guerrillas, who were still continuing to fight for Juárez. The penalty of death was decreed for anyone in Mexico found carrying arms illegally. The sentence was to be carried out within twenty-four hours, and there could be no appeal from it.

Foreign opinion was outraged. The English press, normally courteous and reserved where Maximilian was concerned, uttered some savage criticisms. Washington protested to the French Government without success, but the protest had an unseen effect: Napoleon finally and abruptly realized the emptiness of his dream of a Mexican Empire. Hurriedly he wrote to General Bazaine and urged him to speed up the reorganization of the Mexican army so that the troops could gradually be recalled to France over the next year or two. He continued:

> I hope that the Americans, in spite of their bragging, will not want to go to war with us, but with that danger averted, we must know in what condition we shall be able to leave the country after our departure.

Maximilian was horrified when he heard this news and wrote to Napoleon:

> I must tell Your Majesty that the withdrawal of your troops would undo in a day the work created by three years of patient toil.

About the same time, Maximilian received his first warning from a shrewd friend living in Switzerland, who had advised him in 1860 not to accept the throne of Mexico:

> Make your peace with the Government of Juárez. Send the French army home. Withdraw from Mexico now before it is too late.

In dusty, far-off El Paso, the latest place he had made his headquarters, Juárez smiled grimly on hearing the news. He knew he was safe from his pursuers there. Behind him the border was packed with American troops. For fear of a clash with them, the pursuing French troops had come to a final halt in the blistering and desolate wilds of Chihuahua.

> The tide has turned. From now on it will run strongly in our favor. Soon we will find returning to us those former friends who deserted our cause when times were getting worse. Such men are always the first to sense a political change.

The tragedy of Napoleon's experiment in Mexico continued to unfold. In January, 1865, 8000 French troops returned to France. By April, 1865, it was clear that Maximilian and his empire could not be financed by public investment in Mexico nor by those revenues of the country to which he was entitled. Not even the mineral wealth of Sonora—gold, platinum, silver, mer-

An Endangered Throne

cury, and diamonds—could encourage the average Frenchman to invest any more money in the country.

As soon as he realized how bad things really were, Maximilian disbanded the entire Mexican army of 300,000 men. The troops had been a tremendous expense, and their fighting qualities were becoming uncertain. The soldiers could sense another imminent political change. Many thousands of them were Indians of limited education and narrow loyalties. They all knew that Juárez was a man of their own race, and they were slowly becoming convinced that it was wrong for them to be fighting against him by the side of foreign troops. After being discharged from the army, many of these Indians hastened to join the growing band of guerrillas, who were still causing the French so much trouble and expense.

Back in France there was increasing impatience and resentment toward the continually mounting costs of this never-ending Mexican adventure.

Finally, in the middle of 1865, Bazaine, the great administrator and military leader, the one man who had been able to pacify Mexico, received his orders to return to France. Before his departure he arranged that the expeditionary force should be withdrawn in three more drafts. These were scheduled to take effect in November, 1866, March, 1867, and December, 1867.

In May, 1866, Maximilian seriously considered abdication. The prospect hurt his unyielding pride. He was a courageous man, who scorned the thought of running away from a situation because it was becoming more difficult and dangerous. Yet for the safety of Carlota, as she was known in Mexico, he considered surrendering his throne.

"We are not yet defeated," said Carlota. "Let me go to Paris to plead with Napoleon. Perhaps my presence in France will awaken some interest and sympathy in the hearts of the French people. Explain to me the terms that I must ask the emperor to grant us. In the meantime let us give up all thought of renouncing our throne."

Maximilian's requests were reasonable. He asked that Napoleon continue to meet the cost of a mixed force of 20,000 troops until the end of the year 1867. A sum of 500,000 pesos monthly would have to be paid to the Mexican Govern-

An Endangered Throne

ment so that it could remain solvent. General Douay, who was to succeed General Bazaine, was to be responsible for raising and training a new Mexican army before the end of 1867. Maximilian explained that as France was determined to continue the collection of half of the Customs revenue in order to pay off the small French investors, these requests were the most economical that he could submit.

Poor Carlota was both worried and very nervous when she left Mexico in May, 1866. During the voyage across the Atlantic, she complained to the captain of the steady pounding of the steam-driven engines. She slept badly at night, and her fears increased with every mile that separated her from Maximilian.

It was a tragic misfortune that Carlota arrived in France when a ten-day war between Prussia and Austria had just ended in the utter defeat of the latter country. France was now alarmed at the growing threat of Prussian militarism and beginning to wonder if Prussia might not turn on her during the next year or two.

None of the French statesmen were interested in Carlota. She was merely a beautiful young empress whose throne had cost France too many millions of francs already. Her husband, Maximilian, was an Austrian whose country had put up a disappointing resistance to the Prussian Army.

The Empress Eugénie of France reluctantly consented to grant an audience to the desperate Carlota. They went together to Napoleon's private study. Later Carlota said of the interview:

> I spoke to him for two hours. At one moment I saw him weep. He is in a sickly state and gives the impression of a man who feels himself lost, and who no longer knows what to do nor how to act. . . . This is the explanation of the great power of the ministers who forget that France cannot be governed without a head. . . . He imagines that nothing is done or said now as he wishes and that his authority is unrecognized.

Carlota went next to see the Ministers of War and Finance. To them she proved with indisputable facts and figures that it was impossible for the Mexican Government to manage on its present income. The army alone needed to maintain the throne would cost double the total yearly income of the Government.

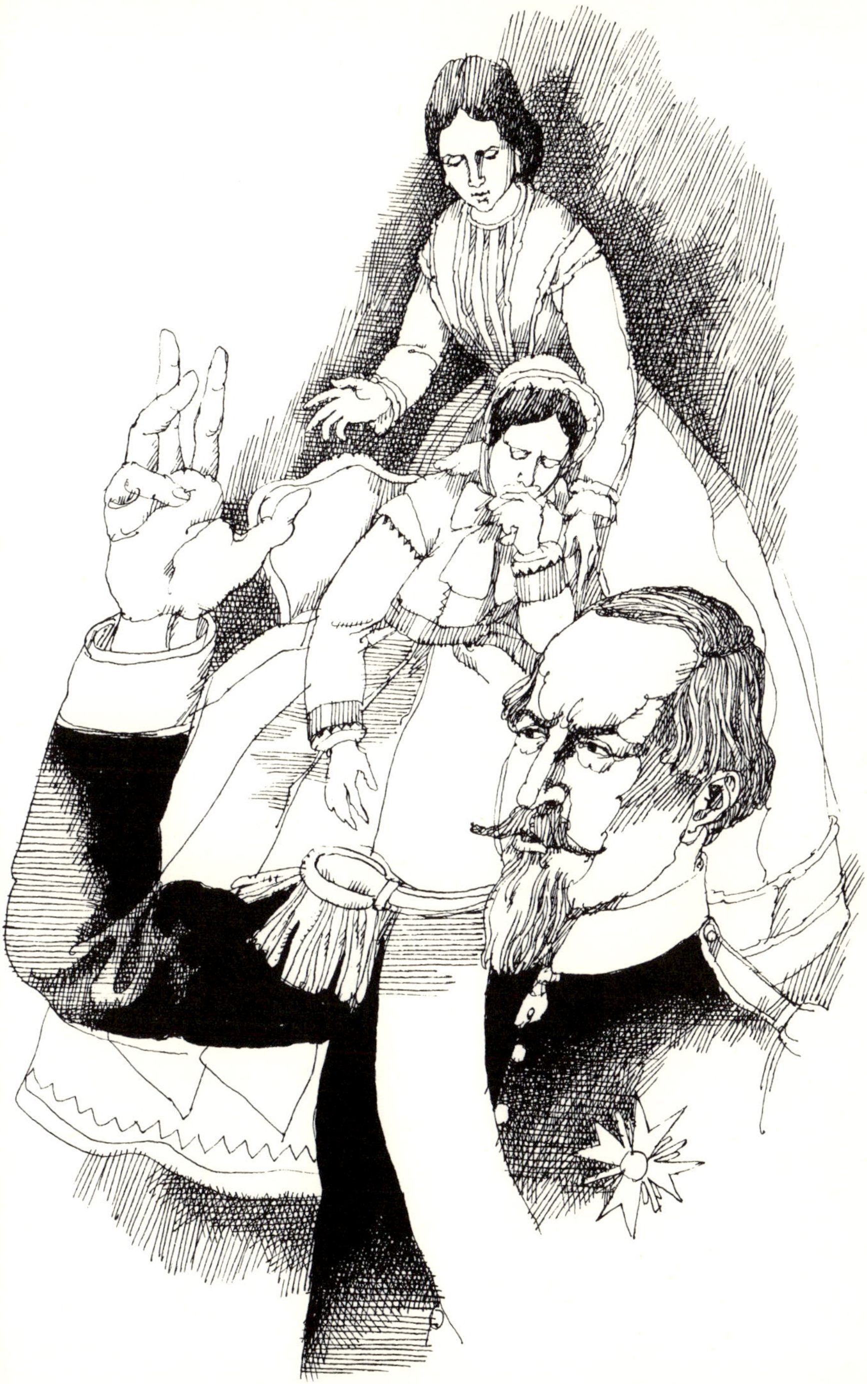

The ministers were polite but evasive. She obtained no satisfaction from them. They refused to comment on her accusations that there had been much graft and corruption in connection with the Mexican loans and investments.

Back went Carlota for one final interview with Napoleon. This time he flatly refused to accede to her desperate requests for more money and for a guarantee that sufficient French troops would remain in Mexico to maintain law and order.

"Then we shall abdicate," declared Carlota. Napoleon nodded. "Abdicate," he said.

Carlota wrote to Maximilian:

> Every word here is a lie. But . . . I told them just what I thought and I stripped them of their masks, but with no lack of courtesy. Certainly nothing so painful has ever happened to them in their lives.

Back to the little castle of Miramar went Carlota, hoping to find there some of the peace she had known in earlier and happier times. Some days later a cable arrived from Maximilian suggesting that she should request an audience of the Pope and try to persuade him to intervene with Napoleon.

To Rome went Carlota, where she was received with much courtesy and honor. Pope Pius IX was seventy-four years old and either unwilling or unable to act as Carlota begged him.

There was no one left to whom the unfortunate empress could turn. Without an army, and without the wealth to pay for one, her husband was alone in Mexico, trying to maintain the throne that she had advised him not to renounce.

Carlota was still in Rome when her tormented mind began to give way under the incessant strain. She was nursed and supervised in her hotel until her brother, the count of Flanders, arrived to take her back to Miramar.

In that quiet castle beside the sea, where she had once known so much happiness, the Archduchess Carlota remained, still beautiful but insane, until her death in 1927.

9 Royal Tragedy

The news of Carlota's tragedy so upset Maximilian that he retired to his private suite and remained alone for several days. When he emerged it was to inform General Bazaine (who had delayed his return to France) that he had decided to abdicate. Without further notification to anyone, he set off at once for Veracruz. He turned aside, however, at the town of Orizaba and found temporary quarters for himself in the Governor's Palace. From there he wrote to Bazaine stating that he wished to annul the law that inflicted the death penalty on anyone found illegally possessing arms. Furthermore, he wrote, there should be no political persecution of any kind, and all hostilities should cease forthwith.

Maximilian's action came too late to save the lives of the fifty or sixty Mexicans who had already been executed by the French. This was to count heavily against the unhappy young man in days to come.

Maximilian certainly intended to abdicate, yet for some reason he could not force himself to take the final step. It might be that he was dazed and shocked by grief and confused in his own mind as to what he should do. All his personal belongings were packed and made ready for transportation to Veracruz. An Austrian warship was lying at anchor in that port, ready to convey him to Europe. Maximilian would have fared better if a kind hand had guided him aboard that vessel and left him to watch the coast of Mexico disappear into the blue haze astern.

It was too late. The ministers of his cabinet followed him from Mexico City. They pleaded with him to return. They promised an advance

Royal Tragedy

of two million Mexican dollars, collected from no one knew where, and enough men to form the nucleus of a new army. A letter arrived from his mother, the empress of Austria. It would be unseemly, declared that regal lady, for any member of the royal Hapsburgs to "leave with the baggage of the French army." It was his duty, she added, "however dangerous it might be, to remain with the Mexican people and to die, if necessary, in the ruins of Mexico City."

The empress was brought up in the stiff traditions of the old-time aristocrats of Europe. Napoleon, who lacked those traditions, believed otherwise. He wrote to Maximilian at Orizaba and advised him strongly to abdicate without delay. Owing to the Prussian threat, added Napoleon, the remaining French troops would have to be withdrawn ahead of schedule.

The unhappy young emperor hesitated for six weeks. He was unwell for most of that time and weary of the ministers, who remained near him at Orizaba. Finally his pride and sense of duty forced him to a decision. He decided not to abdicate; he would make one last try to retain his throne, even after the last of the French departed.

He stuck to that decision even when General de Castelnau, the direct representative of Napoleon, arrived in Mexico to repeat the advice that abdication was both necessary and urgent. On December 1, 1866, Maxmilian announced to the people of Mexico that he would retain the crown until Congress could meet to decide the future of the nation.

General Bazaine held his own blunt views:

> We should destroy all the cannon and munitions we cannot take with us. It will prevent the Conservatives and all those factions who are opposed to Juárez from making use of them in what will be a useless resistance. The forces Juárez is gathering will overcome them in a week. As for the emperor and that arch-bandit, Marquez, whom he has brought back from exile in Europe to fight for his cause, we should kidnap them both. Maximilian for his own sake. Marquez because he has never been anything but a dangerous criminal in Mexico.

Like vultures gathering to feast, once-familiar characters reappeared in Mexico City, each with his own scheme to profit by the impending collapse of the Mexican Empire. Miramón was there

Royal Tragedy

to confer eagerly with Marquez, the safe robber. Old Santa Anna, who had been living in exile since his last disappearance in 1854, returned with the faint hope that somehow he might once again achieve the presidency. General Ortega, who had deserted Juárez in Chihuahua and taken himself off to the American side of the border, suddenly found that his presence in Mexico City was necessary.

Far to the north, in Chihuahua, Juárez's advisers were insisting that he should begin his return to the capital. They pointed out that there were already too many dangerous men gathering in the city to conspire against his government and to plan armed resistance. However, he replied:

> We have resisted the French for five years. What difference does another month or two make? Let us allow General Bazaine the honor of marching out of Mexico City with his troops and with the same dignity they showed when they first marched into the city. When the fruit is about to fall from the tree, it is more comfortable to sit in the shade beneath the branches and wait for a little while. Climbing the tree in a hurry may result in scratches, or even a painful fall.

Juárez was sixty years old. He had put on weight during the past year or two, and his hair had become completely white. But his movements were still brisk, his mind as agile as ever. It was not lethargy that made him postpone his return to Mexico City; he knew that he would win the game with a final move, and he was in no hurry to make it. Much wiser, he thought, to remain until his plans for the future of Mexico were finally complete.

In a letter to his wife, who had gone to New York to visit a sick relative, he wrote:

> Great has been the calamity that has weighed on us in these last years. Now we must consider the future when after this war Mexico will be free of the triple burdens of a Church that interferes with State, of privileged classes, and of tiresome treaties with European powers.

Juárez began his return march at the end of December, 1866. He traveled in a small party consisting of his closest friends and advisers, and for once he made the mistake of underestimating his enemies. He reached the city of Zacatecas, where he was given an enthusiastic public reception. Four days later the city was attacked by Miramón, who with a small force he had somehow managed to scrape together had made a number of forced marches in order to take his old enemy by surprise.

The loyal garrison of Zacatecas managed to hold back the attackers for a few hours. Juárez remained with them until almost the last moment. He finally agreed to save himself only when Miramón's troops were already entering the town.

"Leave my carriage here," he said. "I will be back to claim it before very long."

He swung himself onto a horse and galloped out of the town, followed by his ministers, to whom this means of flight was most unwelcome.

Loyal government troops were hastily brought up by a General Escobedo, who had been selected by Juárez as one of his new commanders. Miramón was forced to make a hasty retreat, whereupon Juárez returned from the hills where he had been hiding out for the past few days.

Margarita Juárez was shocked by her husband's careless attitude toward his own safety. From New York she wrote a scolding letter to him, to which Juárez replied in mild words:

Only my valise was saved from pillage, and also a very handsome walking stick with which the people of Zacatecas had just presented me. . . . There are situations in life when one must risk everything if one wishes to go on living, physically and morally, and I was in those circumstances when the town was attacked. I am through safely and I am satisfied with what I did.

When Miramón retreated, he was forced to leave behind him a number of his secret documents. Among them was an order signed by Maximilian that directed Miramón, if he captured Juárez and his ministers, to try and sentence them by court-martial. However, added Maximilian, the sentence was not to be carried out until the matter had been referred to himself.

This order came as a shock to Juárez. Maximilian had always referred to him with courtesy, had once offered him his old position as president of the Supreme Court, and had stated recently that he was prepared to consider the possible re-election of Juárez to the position of president of Mexico. Yet here was the emperor ordering Miramón, a man who was a mere rebel, to take Juárez before a court-martial. How safe would Juárez's life have been in the hands of a jealous and unscrupulous man such as Miramón, who had plenty of cause to hate him?

Juárez continued his southward journey, an ever-growing army tramping along the dusty roads behind him. The last of the French army marched out of Mexico City on February 5, 1867. A month later the transports bearing the troops sailed away from Mexico. Now Maximilian was left with limited forces of Mexican soldiers, badly armed and of doubtful allegiance, to confront the advancing Juárez.

The emperor chose to make his desperate stand 120 miles north of Mexico City, in the town of Querétaro. He had ignored a last message from Bazaine stating that accommodation could still be offered him aboard one of the transports.

General Escobedo, an exmuleteer, surrounded the city. Maximilian was inside the walls with Miramón, Marquez, and ten thousand men. They held out for four weeks, during which time Marquez, as adroit as ever at looking out for his own skin, contrived to escape on horseback. He left Mexico and never returned. On May 15, a traitor guided the attacking troops into the town through a small and neglected gateway. Maximilian and his staff officers, asleep at their headquarters in the Convent La Cruz, awakened to find themselves prisoners and the city captured.

"I have signed my abdication," Maximilian said to Escobedo, when he was brought before that officer. "I ask that an escort may be given me so that I may leave the country after giving my promise that I will never return to Mexico."

"That is a matter on which the Government will have to decide," replied Escobedo. "For the present I regret the necessity that forces me to detain you."

Maximilian was held with Miramón and one of his principal officers, a bold-faced Indian named Mejia. During this time Juárez avoided any meeting with the former emperor, perhaps because he felt that his sympathetic nature might prompt him to release Maximilian without trial and allow him to leave the country freely. Juárez knew that the charges to be brought against the former emperor were of too serious a nature to permit his personal intervention. These charges stated that Maximilian was a usurper of public power, that he had shown himself as an enemy of independence and of the security of the nation, a violator of international law and the rights of the individual. Weighing most heavily against him was the decree ordering any Mexican bearing arms to be court-martialed and shot.

The trial in Querétaro lasted from the eleventh of June to the fifteenth. Maximilian was ably defended by three lawyers, all of whom were supporters of Juárez, but had volunteered their services freely for the trial. Whatever the normal standards of integrity in Mexican law courts, no one could claim that the trial was anything but strictly honorable. Maximilian himself was not present. He remained proud to the last and refused to appear as defendant in a court. Prepared to die, he would not face public disgrace.

Miramón and Mejia were condemned to death. In a verdict that shocked the entire world, Maximilian was awarded the same penalty.

Tremendous pressure was instantly applied to Juárez, both within Mexico and from outside. The Prussian minister was one of the first to intercede for Maximilian's life. Washington expressed the wish of the president and of the American people that the former emperor be spared. "Harsh measures," added the message, "will not raise the character of the United States of Mexico in the esteem of civilized peoples."

Garibaldi, the great Italian patriot, who had led his country to the gateway of democratic freedom and was much admired in Mexico, made his own personal appeal. The Emperor Franz Joseph did likewise, submitting a simple but dignified plea on behalf of his younger brother. Victor Hugo, the great French poet, dramatist, and novelist, cabled his personal appeal in noble language.

Then there were the Mexicans themselves. In spite of the crimes for which he was convicted, the young Maximilian's imminent death stirred many of them to a generous sympathy that carried them to the gates of the Presidential Palace.

To one high-born woman who clung, weeping, to his knees as she begged that Maximilian's life might be spared, Juárez replied:

> If you were all the kings of Europe, I could not justly intercede on Maximilian's behalf. It is not I who have condemned him to death. It is the law and the people of Mexico. If I turned aside that verdict,

Royal Tragedy 163

the nation would certainly destroy the former emperor themselves and my own life also would be forfeit to them.

There was no doubt that the verdict came to Juárez as a shock that disturbed him as deeply as the pleas for mercy which he received. He was weary of war, weary of killings, and intensely weary of all the useless sacrifices of past years. His heart was filled with an intense longing for peace for himself and the nation, for a few years in which to try to lead the country toward the greater liberty of that democracy, which his countrymen still so little understood and so constantly abused.

Juárez finally broke beneath the strain. He reached a stage where he could no longer endure the tragic appeals, the tears and the touching eloquence of the messages he received. He retired to his private suite in the Palace, shut himself up, and refused to see anyone, even his own ministers, for three whole days. Only one message was brought to him during all that time: a farewell note from Maximilian. After congratulating Juárez on his final victory, Maxmilian wrote:

> May my blood be the last to be shed. Devote that perseverance which you have shown in defending the cause that has just triumphed, a cause that I was glad to recognize and esteem in happier days, to the nobler task of restoring peace to this unfortunate country.

On June 19, 1867, three ill-kept carriages lumbered through the narrow streets of Querétaro, now packed by dense and silent crowds. In each of them stood a lonely figure, Mejia, Miramón, and Maximilian. On reaching the musketry range outside the town where they were to meet their death, Maximilian turned to comfort the weeping priest, who stumbled as they walked together. Then, turning to face the firing squad, he said in a clear, firm voice to the officer in charge:

> I die for a just cause, the cause of the freedom and independence of Mexico. May my blood put an end to the misfortunes of my new country. Long live Mexico!

Juárez emerged from the seclusion of his Palace to find, as he had expected, that by most of the world he was now regarded as a murderer.

Only the working class of France, embittered by ancient tales of the wrongs their forefathers had endured under bygone emperors, found cause to rejoice in Maximilian's death. They were alone in their sentiments. Said the *Moniteur,* one of France's most influential newspapers:

> This infamous act, ordered by Juárez, brands the brows of the men who call themselves the representatives of the Mexican Republic with an ineradicable stain. The scorn of all civilized nations will be the first punishment of the Government which has such a leader at its head.

In Mexico itself, the nation was again hopelessly split. No one could estimate how many there were who detested Juárez for the part he had played in Maximilian's death. Such critics were obliged to remain silent as they bided their time, for the Army leaders and most of the prominent politicians had outwardly favored the verdict. In Mexico it was always dangerous to express one's honest opinion in public. Even those who disapproved found it wiser to line the streets and cheer as Juárez entered Mexico City, for a new star was rising in the Mexican firmament that threatened to overshadow the great Juárez himself.

General Porfirio Díaz was a grim-faced and fiercely mustached young administrative officer who had volunteered his services to Juárez before the flight to Mexico City in 1863. Since then he had remained loyal. He had helped to defeat the French in various skirmishes and gradually risen to his present high rank. He was of mixed Spanish and Indian blood and had been born in Oaxaca in 1830. He was thus twenty-four years younger than Juárez, who had once been his professor at the Civil College in Oaxaca. A cold, deliberate, ruthless man, he was shrewd enough to support the Liberal, or democratic, principles that were now the fashion in Mexico. Yet judging by his later career, Díaz had his own ideas as to how Mexico should be governed.

It was this General Porfirio Díaz who made all the arrangements for the official reentry of Juárez into Mexico City. His secret agents mingled with the crowds lining the Calle de San Francisco, watching and listening for any muttered criticism or disapproving word. Díaz was

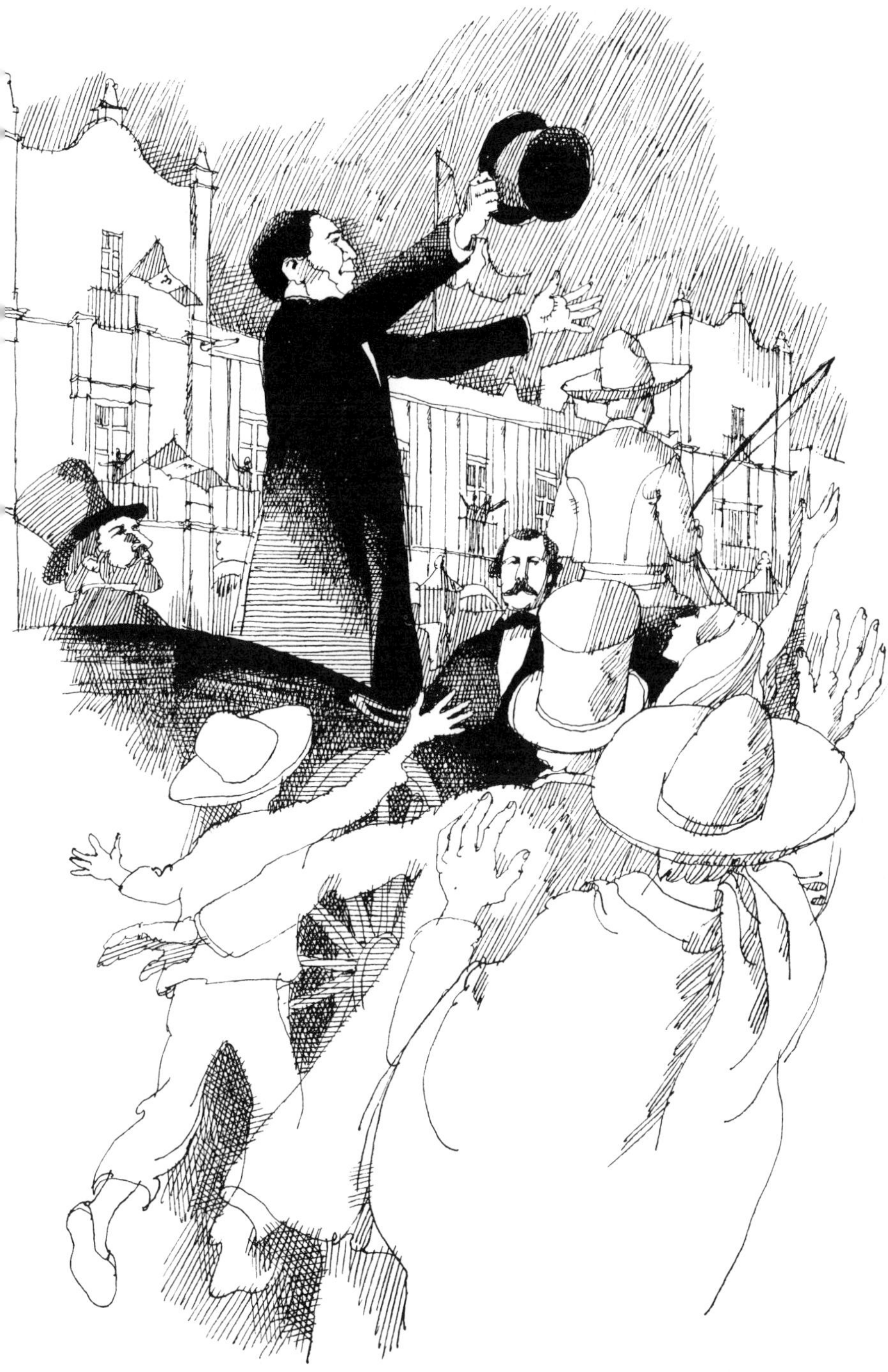

Royal Tragedy

already beginning to exercise his authority over the Mexican people, and Juárez could truthfully write:

> The reception on Monday will be something extraordinary. Tremendous preparations are being made for it in Mexico City.

On that Monday, July 17, 1867, Juárez reached the zenith of his rule as president, the culmination of the struggle for democratic freedom that he had begun ten years earlier. Even those Mexicans who had been shocked by Maximilian's personal tragedy grudgingly admired Juárez for his courage and perseverance, his faith and integrity. In the entire history of Mexico no man had ever enjoyed a comparable record. There was even a remote chance that with the return of peace to the country, Juárez might be able to introduce more progressive reforms. The prosperity he had brought to Oaxaca during his term as governor could perhaps be repeated on a nationwide scale. None of these things were likely, as the Mexicans knew too well, but at least under Juárez they had a Government that was honestly attempting to do its best.

However, the Government was still bankrupt. Years of strife, the national income confiscated by Maximilian and the French, had left Mexico almost devoid of funds. There was not enough money to pay the members of Congress. Government administrative offices were short of pens, ink, and paper. The teachers "were leaving their work to look for a piece of bread." The troops who had defeated the French could not be paid regularly. The revenues from the Customs were vanishing in the same old way by graft and speculation. Taxes and the inevitable dishonesty had ruined most of industry.

Juárez exerted himself to raise money by attempting to enforce the Ley Lerdo. The Church opposed him violently, threatening to stir up widespread trouble at the first confiscation. He called for a general election to terminate or renew his position as president, which he had prolonged by decree in 1865, while he was in exile. He was reelected in that same year of 1867. His popularity was decreasing, however, and the nation opposed him when he tried to introduce certain new clauses into the Constitution, one of which was intended to create an upper house in Congress, and another to allow Federal employees to run for election to Congress.

It was during this more than usually difficult period of Mexican national life that Porfirio Díaz decided to return quietly to his farm in Oaxaca with the remark, "Only a fool stands in a cold stream before he has made up his mind to swim across it."

It was clear to Díaz that Juárez was in for a difficult time after his reelection. All over the country various hotheads were trying to stir up the customary revolts against the Federal Government. The reasons for these rebellions were always vague, but so were the men who led them. The limit of their ambitions was that each man among them wanted to be president for a while, pocket as much wealth as he could, and successfully leave the country on a fast horse before his sins caught up with him. Díaz wanted no part of it. Democracy might serve others well enough if they lacked all personal ambition, but it would not do for him. Thus he preferred to remain absent from the political scene until the time was ripe to make his own bid for power.

Between 1867 and 1870 revolts actually broke

out in nine different states, ranging from Sonora in the north to Yucatán in the southeast. There were the usual shootings of prisoners, demands for ransoms, frantic speeches, and the inevitable hurried departure before the Federal troops arrived. All these revolts came to nothing. They were foolish affairs led by foolish men.

In 1870, Juárez was still in the Presidential Palace and gradually regaining control of the situation. He was now sixty-four years old, and there were signs that "the little Indian" was failing at last. He walked slowly and his back was more stooped. His dark eyes had lost much of their old fire, and even his speeches, which had been hard-hitting and forthright in the old days, were now becoming slow and painstaking. By some he was suspected of increasing tolerance toward the still-powerful Church. In *El Monitor Republicano*, he was openly accused of "the suffocation of his government under a Jesuit's bonnet."

But even the loudest critics were forced to admit, however reluctantly, that Mexico was slowly regaining some slight degree of vigor and that progress was being made in improving social conditions. Matias Romero, the Minister of Finance, was introducing some order into the Treasury. Mexico was still cut off from the disapproving world of Europe, but relations with the United States and the South American countries had never been better. In 1869, diplomatic relations were established with the newly founded North German Confederation and also with Italy, which had always maintained a friendly attitude toward Mexico.

Juárez was using the same methods that he had employed in Oaxaca years earlier to improve conditions in the nation. He insisted on careful economy, built new roads, encouraged the founding of commercial enterprises, and devoted many of the limited funds at the disposal of his government to the creation of new schools. The police were reorganized by some very firm new methods and, despite their protests, a number of incompetent senior officers were sacked. Juárez then turned his attention to the Customs Department, which since time immemorial had been run by dishonest officials largely for their own profit.

After his harsh new measures had been introduced, government revenue from this source increased by twenty-five per cent.

Finally Juárez named as his successor Sebastián Lerdo de Tejada, the younger brother of the great Miguel Lerdo de Tejada, who had framed the famous Ley Lerdo in 1856. Sebastián had shared Juárez's exile in Chihuahua during the French occupation, was an ex-Jesuit who had chosen to support the cause of democracy, and a cultivated man of moderate views who enjoyed a good deal of popularity throughout Mexico.

Porfirio Díaz, busy growing sugarcane in Oaxaca, heard this piece of news without comment. In his white trousers, broad-brimmed hat, and knee boots, he was still creating the impression that he had renounced politics. None of his neighbors suspected that he had done nothing of the sort. He was merely waiting his time and calculating his chances. When Juárez goes, Díaz asked himself, will Sebastián Lerdo, the vice-president be able to control the nation? Would it be better to make a move before Lerdo has had time to take over the presidency and while the administration is still disorganized? Or would it be better to wait until the people grew tired, as they invariably did, of having one president for too long?

While Díaz sat on his farm and considered, Juárez was suffering a fresh misfortune. His devoted wife, Margarita, died at the early age of forty-five. Grief so overcame Juárez that he collapsed. It was to the credit of the Mexican people that even those most bitterly opposed to the Federal Government forgot their animosities and demonstrated their sympathy in unexpected ways. Two ringleaders of recent revolts whom Juárez had pardoned, Aureliano Rivera and Miguel Negrete, volunteered to act as pallbearers. A public demonstration scheduled to take place in Zacatecas was postponed until after the funeral. The opposition newspapers were as eloquent in their expressions of mourning as the section of the press that supported Juárez. The funeral procession in Mexico City passed before silent crowds who had lined the streets to demonstrate their sympathy.

Alone and showing increasing signs of age, Juárez returned to his immense task of developing the country. Even though England, like the rest of the European countries, refused to recognize

Mexico, an English construction company was building a railroad between Veracruz and Mexico City. Another railway was about to be built across the northwest area of Mexico. Plans were being finalized for the construction of another line across southern Mexico to the port of Tehuantepec. An American shipping company had begun plying to Yucatán, and there was even some talk of a railroad that would run all the way from California to Panama. Mexico was at last beginning to go ahead. If the nation could only keep clear of the needless insurrections that had so often destroyed it in past years, prospects for the future would remain brighter than they had ever been before.

Opponents in Congress declared that they were not satisfied with all that was being done.

"The Constitution states that all Mexicans shall be equal," they fretted. "How can this equality exist when such a large proportion of our nation is devoured by debt, ignorance, and poverty? A few score of Mexicans own most of the territory of the Republic; the vast majority own nothing at all. In almost every village the inhabitants must work for the landlord in return for tiny and inadequate wages. All commercial enterprise is being stifled by ignorance, lack of capital, and the inability of the workers to adapt themselves to regular hours of labor and to learn new methods and skills. In this country of ours there are nine million people, of whom seven million are Indians who neither buy nor sell anything to assist commerce and industry. Thus two million people must pay all the taxes and maintain the economic and administrative life of Mexico."

Juárez agreed with these criticisms, saying:

> For the past sixty years Mexico has had one political crisis after another. On top of that we have endured militarism in one form or another for the same length of time. The whole country is sick to its soul. No man can hasten the convalescent period. I pray that we may enjoy much-needed peace in the years ahead. Not in the lifetime, perhaps, of the loudest critics alive today will the nation grow strong and prosperous. Our grandchildren may live to see such an era, but in the meantime we must continue to watch over Mexico as the strength of the country gradually increases from day to day.

Juárez was right, but few politicians agreed with him. Most of them held the absurd view that if only the right leader could be found, Mexico in some mysterious way would be restored to prosperity, and her various ills would miraculously disappear overnight. An increasing number of those politicians were beginning to believe that Juárez was not the leader the nation needed. He was growing too old, he had been in politics too long, he was too anxious to smooth over difficulties.

In the general election of 1871, sixty-five-year-old Juárez again ran for president. Porfirio Díaz suddenly appeared from the country and announced that he intended to run as a rival candidate.

This forty-one-year-old general and politician was becoming very popular. Too often the voters of Mexico had listened to a man's fiery speeches and impassioned language instead of coolly surveying his past record and studying his actions. They did the same on this occasion. Many of them had forgotten by this time that Díaz had risen through his friendship with Juárez and that he had once been the faithful ally of the president. Few voters paused to ask themselves if a man who had already changed sides once was a man to whom they could entrust the presidency of the country. Instead they listened to his passionate speeches and nodded approval. They recalled that Díaz had risen from an insignificant inn beside an obscure street in Oaxaca City and forced himself successfully into Mexico's feudal military caste. A man who could do that, reasoned the voters, would undoubtedly make a first-class president, like Juárez, who had also come from humble beginnings. It was a pity that they did not reflect as cautiously as they had done during the dark days when the name of Juárez was first becoming known.

"The name of Porfirio Díaz," said *El Monitor Republicano*, "is a prodigious, magnetic talisman, which sweeps the masses into delirium." How true! When the election had taken place and the votes were counted, it was found that Juárez just lacked an absolutely clear majority. Congress was left to decide the actual winner. There were rumors that the election had been fraudulent, that Díaz had received more votes than Juárez. This was nothing new in Mexico; similar rumors always circulated after every election and they were frequently right.

Juárez was finally named president. Sebastián Lerdo regained his position as vice-president. Critics murmured that it was a mistake for Juárez to have been chosen. He had been necessary in 1861 to hammer the first principles of democracy into the heads of the people. He had been necessary in 1867 as a rebuke to the French invaders and in recompense for his great services to Mexico during his years of exile. Now a new generation had reached maturity. The old man was out of date. He should have retired at the height of his power, to take his place beside those two other great leaders, Washington and Bolívar. He was, they felt, on the way out, but he refused to recognize it.

A revolt broke out in Mexico City on the day that Congress declared Juárez elected. While dangerous mobs roamed the streets, the police mutinied and took the side of the rioters. Several hundred prisoners were freed from the Belém penitentiary and provided with firearms. Mass hysteria had broken loose once again in the capital city.

Juárez made one of his last public appearances.

He emerged from the Palace and stood in the handsome main entrance while he calmly surveyed the rioting crowds.

"We lack orders, sire," said a young officer of the Palace Guards. "General Rocha has not yet appeared to take command, and my men are growing confused."

"That won't do at all," replied Juárez. "I must take the responsibility of command until the general appears."

He walked briskly to the head of the wavering soldiers. His movements were agile, his gaze unfaltering. For a few moments he paused to survey the littered streets, the smashed shops, and the surging crowd.

"It won't do at all," he repeated. "Once again the militarism of the old days has raised its detestable pennant in defiance of the banner of law and order. . . . The Palace Guard will advance!"

The soldiers began to tramp forward to the wide marble steps leading down to the dangerous street. At that moment General Rocha, a portly man with a walrus mustache and merciless eyes, came hastening forward.

"My deep apologies, sire," he exclaimed. "I was sipping chocolate with an official of the Palace when the riot began. Allow me."

Rocha gently urged the president to one side and moved into the place he had been occupying. Juárez turned away and reentered the Palace.

"No prisoners," ordered Rocha, as the troops reached the street. "We are outnumbered and can't spare the men to guard them."

With rifle and bayonet the Palace Guard began to clear the San Cosme. Half a mile further along, they were joined by 4000 loyal troops who had been hurriedly brought into the city. The order of "No prisoners" was repeated to these reinforcements. It was the type of militarism that Mexico had always endured. Human life was cheap.

In his presidential office, Juárez was issuing fresh orders. He knew who had stirred up this revolt and he knew, too, that it was his former friend, Díaz, who had laid most of the plans for it. When the riot ended in Mexico City at the cost of 1000 dead, General Rocha was given orders to march against Oaxaca State, where a mass revolt was expected to begin at any time.

Porfirio Díaz had miscalculated. The population of Oaxaca had not yet decided to revolt. They refused to echo his battle cry of "Porfirio or Death."

His handsome estate in flames, his brother Félix beaten to death by angry villagers armed with sticks and stones, Porfirio Díaz fled from Oaxaca and was swallowed up in the unending emptiness of the vast sierras.

Grimmer and more silent now, alone and growing harsh in his ways, Juárez still retained his presidency. Perhaps it was true that he would have fared better had he resigned. His voluntary retirement would have regained for him the respect and affection of the older generation and evoked the admiration of those who were too young to remember him in his greatest days.

Or was he perhaps right to remain in office? Juárez knew the Mexican people too well. Once he stepped down, they were sure to be at each other's throats again. All the foundations of national development and future prosperity were slowly being laid. Every day that he remained as president those plans became a little further advanced. Fresh troubles would destroy them.

"I am the State," Juárez once said bluntly. "Without me Mexico will falter and fail."

His critics held a different opinion. "Juárez is moving back with giant strides," they declared. "He is returning to the past. In his period of triumph he was surrounded by pure Liberals, men of broad-minded and progressive outlook. Today he is friendly with the Moderates, who have fewer of those qualities. Tomorrow he will be in the hands of the Conservatives, who wish to restore feudalism to Mexico. Farewell to the Constitution!"

Death struck at last.

Late on the night of July 17, 1872, the sixty-seven-year-old Juárez began to feel unwell while working in his private office. He returned to his Palace suite, and at dawn the next morning his personal physician was called.

Juárez suddenly opened his eyes and gazed up at the doctor. "Is my illness fatal?" he asked bluntly.

"Yes, sire, it grieves me very deeply to inform you that it is."

"Then I must see the vice-president at once," said Juárez. "Please inform Señor Sebastián Lerdo that I must discuss some matters with him without delay."

Throughout the interview that followed, Juárez remained seated at his desk, pausing every now and then as a fresh wave of weakness passed over him. When he had finished with Lerdo, he spent another half hour in discussion with General Rocha.

At four o'clock in the afternoon he retired to his bed. "Give me a hand, Camilo," he said to his long-faithful Indian servant. "It is perhaps the last service you will be able to render for me."

Before the bells of the cathedral struck five o'clock that same afternoon, President Benito Pablo Juárez was dead.

DÍAZ

What Happened Afterward

Sebastián Lerdo de Tejada succeeded to the presidency. He granted a general amnesty which, by its terms, enabled Porfirio Díaz to return from his uncomfortable sanctuary in the mountains. Lerdo then called for a general election and went to the trouble of dispatching a courteous telegram to Díaz to notify him that he was free to run for election if he wished.

The nation-wide support of Lerdo was over-

What Happened Afterward

whelming. The average Mexican voter was at last beginning to realize the benefits of a stable and democratic government. They suspected that any government led by Díaz would be very different in its ways and certainly a lot less democratic.

The nation was right. During Lerdo's presidency, the progress that Juárez had foreseen continued. The Mexico-Veracruz railway was opened. Much of the banditry that had always existed in Mexico was firmly suppressed. The Church was finally and emphatically separated from the State, to which it now became subservient. Diplomatic relations were renewed with Spain. A year or so later they were also resumed with France, a country now weakened by a disastrous war against Prussia in 1870. (This defeat compelled Napoleon to abdicate. He retired to England as an exile, where he died in 1873.)

Díaz again returned to his farming, but he continued to brood over his humiliation and defeat. During that time he became a partner in a sugar plantation, built furniture and boats, hunted and fished, and again created the impression that he was done with politics.

In 1876, when Lerdo ran once more for election as president, Díaz led another revolt. After some dramatic adventures and extraordinary escapades, during which Lerdo was declared reelected, Díaz had collected a following of malcontents, bandits, and outlaws strong enough to overcome the government forces. He was installed as president in 1877. Lerdo went into exile in New York and died there in 1890.

Except for one brief period, Díaz remained the dictatorial president of Mexico until 1911. During those thirty-four years he thrust the country back into another period of feudalism. Foreign capitalists were encouraged to create new investments throughout the country. Workers were paid starvation wages, but the investors and the ministers grew rich on the profits. The wealthy aristocrats and churchmen breathed freely again, for Díaz was their faithful friend. As the booming sugarcane estates expanded ever further, labor conditions became almost indistinguishable from slavery. Democracy in Mexico was forgotten.

Díaz went into voluntary exile in France in 1911. By that time, as he knew, the Mexican nation was growing restless as the people recalled the lost freedom for which their fathers had fought under Juárez. Within a year or two of his departure, civil war was imminent. Then followed a period of conflict as bitter as any Mexico had ever experienced in earlier days.

Bibliography

Beals, Carleton, *Porfirio Díaz*. Philadelphia, J. B. Lippincott Co., 1932.
Blanchot, Charles, *Mémoires. L'Intervention française au Mexique*. Paris, Bertrand, 1911.
Johnson, William W., *Heroic Mexico, the Violent Emergence of a Modern Nation*. Garden City, N.Y., Doubleday & Co., 1968.
Paz, Octavio, *The Labyrinth of Solitude*. New York, Grove Press Inc., 1961.
Reed, John, *Insurgent Mexico*. New York, D. Appleton & Co., 1914.
Roeder, Ralph, *Juárez and His Mexico*. New York, Viking Press, 1947.

ABOUT THE AUTHOR

Ronald Syme's early days were spent in an old castle in his native Ireland. Before he was nine he had the free run of the library in his home, thereby acquiring a love of reading. In later boyhood, he spent a few years in New Zealand, mostly hunting wild pig and trout fishing with his sports-loving father. At eighteen he went to sea and visited many parts of the world. About the same time he began writing short stories and feature articles. In 1934 he left the sea to become a journalist. During World War II Mr. Syme first served as ship's gunner, but later transferred to the British Army Intelligence Corps in which he saw service in North Africa, Italy, and Europe.

Today Ronald Syme, a well-known author in both England and the United States, lives in the peaceful South Pacific island of Rarotonga. His home is a century-old, white-walled stone house within two hundred yards of a beautiful lagoon. The shelves of his library are lined with books, and he can check almost any historical fact he needs for his writing. He enjoys, he says, "most of the advantages of civilization without the corresponding disadvantages."